How to Keep Jellyfish in Aquariums

An introductory guide
for maintaining healthy jellies

Chad L. Widmer

How to Keep Jellyfish in Aquariums: An Introductory Guide for Maintaining Healthy Jellies

Published by Wheatmark®
610 East Delano Street, Suite 104
Tucson, Arizona 85705 U.S.A.
www.wheatmark.com

International Standard Book Number:
978-1-60494-126-5

Library of Congress Control Number:
2008927378

In Memory of Clyde D. Widmer, MSG.

He loved his family and country,
music, motorcycles, and fireworks,
and I miss him.

Also

To all my friends present, past, and beyond …

TABLE OF CONTENTS

Remember to make gravity your friend
and that it pays in the long run to be patient
with all things jellyfish.

Part 1: **Getting Started**

Part 2: **Jelly Keeping**

Part 3: **Collections Management**

Part 4: **Culture Work**

Appendices

ACKNOWLEDGMENTS

HEARTFELT THANKS ARE due to A. Pereyra, S. Wright, and T. Knowles, good friends who took time from their busy schedules to read the manuscript and offer valuable suggestions. Their candor and honest feedback greatly improved the content and quality of the book. I also would like to thank all of the C. Widmers, my family, for their support and guidance during this project. I would like to thank the Monterey Bay Aquarium for all of the treasured opportunities. The photos included in the book are from behind the scenes and are credited to the Monterey Bay Aquarium, copyright 2008. I wish to sincerely thank senior staff at the Monterey Bay Aquarium for granting me permission to use my photos gratis. I would also like to thank the animals for being inherently interesting, and I thank Neptune and Davy Jones for being kind to me when I am at sea. Finally, it should be known that I very much appreciate the U.S. Army college fund and Humboldt State University for the education that allowed me to do this work.

INTRODUCTION

W HEN I STARTED writing this guide, I was a senior aquarist at the Monterey Bay Aquarium
in Monterey, California, working with jellyfish for
nearly eight years. During that time I heard a lot of
"how do I keep and grow jellyfish?" questions. Other
aquarists, researchers, students, and entrepreneurs
were all keenly interested. It seemed there were a lot
of people with similar questions and no easy place
to find the answers. The scientific literature contains
clues about jellyfish husbandry, but the language can
be cryptic for the uninitiated, and the references can
be tricky to track down without access to a well-
stocked university library. The need for a manual in-
troducing jellyfish husbandry from the perspective of
a seasoned jellyfish aquarist was apparent.

The purpose of this guide is to present in plain
language some proven methods for keeping healthy
jellyfish in aquariums. These techniques have served
me well through the years. While this handbook

contains many useful tips and tricks, it is by no means all-inclusive. It is the first manual of its kind that I know of, and subsequent editions will contain more information. The basic principles of jelly-keeping are the same in a public aquarium, a research institution, or in your home. With some studying, attention to detail, and pioneer spirit, you will soon be on the jelly-master path.

••
Throughout the book you will see areas of text set aside in breaks like this one. These are key points and useful tips.
••

Assumptions about the Reader

I assume this is not your first aquarium and that you know about water quality, lighting, and filtration. There are a lot of good resources to be found in pet stores, online, and in the scientific literature. One of my favorite references is *The Marine Aquarium Handbook: Beginner to Breeder* by Martin Moe.

I also assume you realize there is a learning curve and that you are unlikely to be successful with your very first batch of jellies but will soon become good at it. Keeping jellyfish requires a bit of intuition, and jelly intuition takes time to develop. With practice and patience, the number of jellyfish species you are able to care for will increase.

Right now, keeping jellyfish is for advanced aquarists, not because the work is difficult or hard to understand but because the life-support system requires daily attention and appropriate responses from the aquarist for success. No problem; I explain the most common issues that occur and how to fix them.

If you want to build your own jelly-keeping life-support system, I assume that you know your way around the hardware shop a bit, or at least you're not afraid to go inside the store and ask for the parts you need.

How the Book Is Organized

The book is divided into five sections. The first part of the manual covers what you need to know in order to get started quickly, including water quality, suggested jellyfish diets, and tank designs. Part 2 contains useful suggestions for successfully growing some of the most commonly displayed jellies. Part 3 offers tips on collections management for those keeping several different species. Part 4 has to do with starting and maintaining cultures for both scyphomedusae and hydromedusae. Part 5 is comprised of the appendices with information that I have found to be useful through the years. Depending on your experience, you can start reading wherever you'd like.

Using the Words "Jellies" versus "Jellyfish"

In this manual I use the terms "jellyfish," "jelly," and "jellies" interchangeably. When most people think of a jellyfish, they think about a medusa stage that pulses around in the middle of the water column. Sometimes medusae sting when they accidentally bump into people. In that example, using the word "jellyfish" is entirely appropriate. There are some folks out there who eagerly point out that one term is more

xvi   introduction

correct than another. They usually base the premise of their argument on the fact that jellyfish aren't actually fish because they don't possess the same kind of gills that fish do and so on. And I respectfully point out to them that jellies aren't actually made up of "jelly" either, in the same way that starfish aren't exactly made up of cosmic burning balls of gas.

Deciding which term to appropriately use has to do with the taxonomy of the animal being discussed. Medusae belonging to the phylum Cnidaria are properly referred to as jellyfish. There are a lot of other animals in the ocean with gelatinous bodies belonging to lots of other phyla, or groups of animals. A few examples are swimming snails (phylum Mollusca), salps (phylum Chordata) and segmented worms (phylum Annelida). Animals that do not belong to the phylum Cnidaria but do possess gelatinous bodies are referred to by specialists as jellies, gelatinous zooplankton, or gelata. You would be technically correct calling a Cnidarian medusa a jelly or a jellyfish, but to be strictly accurate you would call a swimming Chordate (a salp) a jelly but not a jellyfish.

Responsible Jellyfish Keeping

There are a few ethical issues to consider when growing jellies. The most important ones have to do with acquisition and de-acquisition. If you decide to collect your own specimens, make sure you have the proper permits. Laws vary from state to state, so it's possible that you aren't required to possess a permit, but it is better to check and get one rather than pay a hefty fine and have your collecting gear confiscated.

Responsible releasing is a must in order to prevent the spreading of nonnative jellyfish.

Non-native jellyfish are ones that normally live in one part of the world and have somehow been introduced somewhere else. They can have drastic negative effects on their new ecosystems because they often eat the foods other animals depend on. Therefore, to responsibly de-acquire jellyfish, you might first try giving them to another jelly keeper. Another option is to cull them humanely in a bag of seawater left overnight in the freezer. Dispose of dead jellies in the garbage or send them down a drain leading to the sewer, but *do not* dump live or dead ones into a neighboring body of seawater. Dispose of used jelly seawater in the sewer because the sewer leads to the waste water treatment plant. Their systems should kill any unseen larval stages that may be present in the water.

Before you dump large quantities of seawater into the sewer, I recommend that you contact your local wastewater treatment facility to make sure that your routine maintenance won't have any deleterious effects on your community's water supply. Contacting the wastewater treatment plant folks is the responsible thing to do. It is important because some plants reclaim the water as irrigation water for farm crops. If agricultural crops are irrigated with salt water, they generally die.

Part 1
Getting Started

1

WATER AND LIFE-SUPPORT SYSTEMS

Water Quality

HEALTHY CAPTIVE JELLYFISH require excellent water quality. Fortunately, one can use either natural or artificial seawater for jelly keeping. I won't go into all of the details of how to treat or make artificial seawater in this guide because there are plenty of other resources available online and in other books. But treat the water in your jelly habitat as you would treat a living organism. Healthy jelly-system water should be well cared for, with all the necessary elements in proper proportion, and maintained at an appropriate temperature. Different jellyfish species have different tolerances for seawater conditions ranging outside of their normal operating conditions. Below I briefly discuss the consequences of exceeding water quality parameters with commonly kept jellies.

All jellies have an optimal temperature range in which they can be maintained and remain healthy. When deciding on water temperature, it is better to accidentally set the temperature too low to start. If the temperature is too high for over forty-eight hours, enzymes inside the jellies can get bent out of shape. Affected jellies evert their bells (looking like a blown-out umbrella in a wind storm) and have up to a 90% mortality rate. If the temperature is too low, the enzymes are spared, but the jellyfish pulse less, feed less, and metabolize food more slowly, leading to slow or reversed growth. Fortunately, if you realize that the temperature is too low, you can increase it by a few degrees, and the jellyfish generally recover.

> •••
>
> If you choose to collect your own seawater from the ocean I highly recommend that when transporting your water home you use tied-down recycled water jugs with secure lids for the trip. I once used garbage pails with lids that weren't very secure to transport seawater. I had painstakingly carried seawater-filled buckets over sharp, jetty rocks while dodging waves at the Humboldt Bay jetty. I arrived safely at my truck, but on the way home I took a corner a little too sharply, accidentally spilling about 200 gallons and creating a mini-tsunami on the freeway.
>
> •••

The average salinity of seawater used for growing most kinds of jellyfish is about 33 parts per thousand (also known as practical salinity units, or PSU). If the salinity in your jellyfish system is too low, jellyfish may go downhill due to osmotic stress. Species living in estuaries are far more tolerant of fluctuating salinity than their open-ocean counterparts. Jellies that are exposed to a high salinity and then returned to appropriate levels generally recover. Therefore, it is important to monitor the salinity levels in your system daily and make appropriate adjustments. In lighted, warm-water life-support systems, water tends to evaporate quickly, so it is often necessary to add fresh water to make up for what is lost due to evaporation.

• •

Keep track of your recipes for growing a particularly good batch of jellies and try to duplicate and improve upon them over time (e.g., "I kept a good group of Japanese moon jellies at 34 ppt, 15°C, and fed them nauplii and small krill …").

• •

Comparatively speaking, jellyfish are more tolerant of lower oxygen concentrations for extended periods than are fish. Having a high tolerance for low oxygen concentrations is good news when shipping jellyfish because they can get by with low oxygen in their shipping bags for a few days at a time. Likewise, systems that are supersaturated with oxygen tend to be bad for some jellies. Oxygen can come out of solution inside the jellies' gut canals and cause internal bubbles. Excessive oxygen can also be toxic to some jellies, which is manifested as many small holes or pits on their bells.

Keep track of important happenings in your jellyfish system. It is a good idea to keep a log book next to the system in order to record feeding times and amounts, performed maintenance, and water quality parameters and times (e.g., salinity, temperature, dissolved oxygen, date of last water change, etc.). A good log book can help you unravel the mystery of why a cohort of jellyfish did particularly well or poorly.

Basic Life-Support System Components to Consider

Life-support systems for jellyfish aquariums are similar to life-support systems in most other aquaria. In the simplest jellies system, there is a reservoir for holding water and a main jellies display tank. An electric pump in the reservoir sends water to the various components of the system much like the heart of a living organism. Water is pumped from the reservoir to a chiller (if required), which then returns water to the reservoir. Water is also sent to the jellyfish display tank. After the water circulates through the display tank, it returns to the reservoir after first passing through a trickle filter and a bag filter. Protein skimmers don't belong in your jellyfish system. There is growing evidence supporting the idea that jellyfish can use dissolved organic materials obtained directly from the water. A protein skimmer may rob the jellyfish of food.

If water goes into a jellyfish tank, then water also has to leave the tank. The general idea of water movement in jelly tanks is to generate enough current to keep the jellies up and off the bottom of the tank without having them get sucked out of the tank as water leaves. Water leaves the display tank through an outflow port (hole where water exits the tank); most outflow ports are covered with some kind of screen mechanism to keep jellies from leaving the display tank along with the water returning to the reservoir. Several neat tricks have been developed to keep jellies from sticking to the screens covering the drainage ports. Some of the most common methods are laminar flow plates, spray bars, and air bubbles. What these are and how they work are discussed in the next chapter.

2

BASICS OF TANK DESIGN AND FUNCTION

The Bottom Line with Holding Tanks . . .

I'M GOING TO let you in on something I stumbled across while committing science one day. You can grow jellyfish in a bathtub so long as you have excellent water quality, good food, and keep the currents adjusted properly. If you have any kind of outflow current leaving the display tank, whether it is going down to a reservoir or into a power head intake, you need to somehow keep jellyfish away from the outflow and prevent them from getting caught in the suction source. Meanwhile, you must also keep them from getting beaten up by excessive currents in the tank while keeping them suspended. An active imagination can design all sorts of different methods for preventing jellies from getting stuck to suction sources.

Glass Culture Dishes (fig. 3.1A)

Culture dishes may be purchased from a scientific supply store online, or you can use small glass dishes or jars from around the house. Make sure the dishes are clean before using them. Dishes are employed with or without magnetic stir bars, depending on the husbandry requirements of the jellies being grown.

Most commercial air- or water-driven magnetic stirrers operate when water or air spins a plate with a magnetic strip attached. The plate spins underneath the dish. The seawater-filled dish sitting on top of the spinning plate contains jellies and a small magnet. As the plate spins under the dish, the magnet inside the dish also spins, thus stirring the water. Magnets are produced in different shapes and sizes, ranging from pill-shaped to plus-shaped magnets. I prefer the plus-shaped ones to the pill-shaped ones.

••

If a vortex forms in the middle of the dish, the stirrer is probably spinning too fast. When adjusting the spinning rate of the magnet, keep it low enough to get the jellies up and off the bottom of the dish without bouncing them around wildly.

••

Pros: Glass dishes are an inexpensive and versatile rearing vessel for delicate species.

Cons: Maintenance requires daily water changes. It is easy to overfeed and foul the water, which will kill the jellies.

Screened-in Flow-through Tanks (fig. 3.1B and fig. 3.1C)

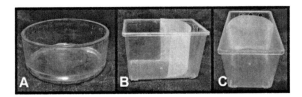

Figure 3.1. A standard glass culture dish (A). They are sold in several sizes. I most often use four- and eight-inch diameter glass dishes. The four-inch dishes are used for keeping cultures of jellyfish polyps (scyphistomae), and I use the eight-inch dishes for raising juvenile medusae. Screened-in flow-through tank, side view (B). Top view, looking down and into the tank (C). Screened-in flow-through tanks are often used as juvenile jellyfish catch tanks and small medusa grow-out tanks. Water gently enters from a tube fastened to the side of the tank, circulates, and then passes though the large arc shaped screen as it leaves the tank and returns to the reservoir.

The arc-shaped (parabolic) screen allows water leaving the tank to pass through lots of little holes instead of one large hole. Therefore, suction at the outflow screen is diffused over a large surface area, and jellies have less chance of becoming stuck. It is a good idea to place an air line with large, slow, and gently flowing bubbles near the outflow screen in order to generate tank currents and keep jellies from sticking to the screen. Use a single weight on the bottom of the airline.

Pros: Overfeeding is less of a problem than when using a standing dish of water.
Cons: The screens should be brushed every other day.

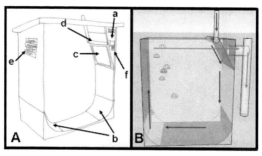

Figure 3.2. A one-foot diameter pseudokreisel and its
components: outflow port (A); bottom curves (B); screen (C);
spray bar (D); jellyfish tank report card (E); return-to-reservoir
drain (F). The companion illustration shows a functioning
pseudokreisel.

Pseudokreisels

Pseudokreisels are used for growing most species
discussed in this guide; they are one my favorite tank
styles because of their versatility and forgivingness.
They are called pseudo or "false" kreisels because the
water currents in the tank are generated through a
spray bar with incoming water only—the currents are
not generated by electric pumps, as are the currents
in *eu* or "true" kreisels. A spray bar is a single, straight
bar with small holes drilled into it, all situated in a
straight line, one next to the other (fig. 3.2D). Spray
bars are positioned so water going through them
gently pushes jellies away from the outflow screen. In
figure 3.2B, the black arrows represent incoming water, which first enters through a spray bar then passes
down the length of the right side of the tank, moving
along the bottom, then upward on the left. The gray
arrows represent water after having encountered jellyfish, which passes through the screen and returns
down to the reservoir.

Pros: They are versatile and inexpensive. You can grow a lot of different kinds of jellyfish in a pseudokreisel. Even better, you can build one yourself (see appendix, fig. A2).

Cons: Pseudokreisels need to be thoroughly cleaned every six weeks or so.

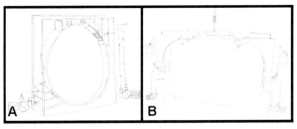

Figure 3.3. Standard kreisel shapes: round kreisel (A) and stretch kreisel (B).

••

You should never use a fine mist–style airstone in a jellies tank. The small bubbles will become trapped inside the gut canals of the jellies and cause them to float. Left untreated, the jellies will perish.

••

Kreisels

Kreisels get their name from a German word for a child's toy spinning top. The name links the spinning motion of the toy to the movement of the water currents inside a tank. But do not make the mistake of setting the current speed in your tank to match that of a top—you'd have dead jellyfish for sure! Kreisels are versatile tanks that are most often manufactured as four- and five-foot diameter round tanks (fig. 3.3A). They may also be stretched out, and then they are referred to as stretch kreisels (fig. 3.3B). Many exhibit tanks at large aquariums are kreisels or modified kreisels. Kreisels make use of laminar flow plates that gently blow jellies away from the suction near outflow screens. A laminar flow plate resembles several drinking straws placed side by side and glued together (a good way to make your own by the way). The flow plate is positioned so that it gently blows water over the entire screen over the water outlet.

> **Pros:** They are good for holding and growing larger jellies and usually have large viewing windows that allow for display, research, and health assessment.
>
> **Cons:** They can be expensive and may be cost-prohibitive. Some parts of the kreisel are difficult to access for repairs.

No two jellyfish display tanks perform exactly alike (except for glass culture dishes). Three "identical" units will probably not be equally good at growing jellyfish. There are many reasons for this. Sometimes the spray bar holes are not equidistantly drilled, or the spray bars may be glued at slightly different angles, thus sending jellyfish in weird trajectories. If the tank was sloppily glued together, water currents will be affected. So if the tank is really performing poorly, I suggest taking the major components apart, cleaning them well, and regluing them.

A tool I like using when managing large numbers of jelly tanks and species is the jellyfish tank grow-out report card. If a jellyfish tank does a particularly good job at growing one kind of jellyfish, I make a note using white electrical tape and a black permanent marker and then affix it to the tank (fig. 3.2E). It is sort of a motivational award for the tank and a reminder for me that this is a good tank for growing more challenging animals.

Balancing Currents in Jelly Tanks

Having properly adjusted currents in your tank is crucial for healthy jellies. The idea is to keep the jellies up and off the bottom of the tank without bouncing them off the walls. One of the common mistakes in jelly keeping begins when the aquarist observes jellies drifting by the viewing window only occasionally. A first impulse may be to increase the current in order to get the jellies moving, thinking they will pass by the viewing window more often. However, increasing the flow usually only exacerbates the problem because the jellies end up scraping off their skin as they bump into the walls of the tank. How to properly adjust tank currents in pseudokreisels and kreisels:

1. *Turn off incoming water and watch your jellies*. Observe their positions in the tank. Where do they accumulate? Take note: do they sink to the bottom, or are they at the top?

2. *Gently add a small amount of current and observe the effects*. Wait at least twenty to thirty minutes after each adjustment before making another one. It takes time for the full effects of minor current adjustments to manifest themselves be-

cause water has momentum. Observe the results of your action. Did the jellies get off the bottom? Did they leave the surface and start to circulate? Are the jellies positioned properly (as in fig. 3.4)?

3. *Gradually increase the current every twenty to thirty minutes until the proper jellyfish placement is achieved.* Remember, the jellies should be up and off the bottom but not rocketing around the perimeter.

> •
> When balancing the currents, make sure not to feed the jellies for twenty-four hours beforehand. Unfed jellies extend their tentacles and oral arms, whereas jellies that are eating retract them, affecting their placement in the tank.
> •

If you are experiencing current control problems in a jelly tank, more often than not the correct answer to the problem is to decrease the flow, not increase it. This is partly because when one increases the incoming water to generate currents and suspend jellies, one also increases the amount of water leaving the tank. The situation results in increased outflow suction at the outflow screen. Something else to try when dealing with flow issues in the tank is changing the direction of water currents. Try setting gentle currents in opposing directions to achieve optimal jellyfish placement. Sometimes the answer to current troubles can be as simple as removing the kreisel lid.

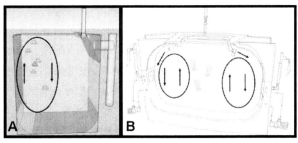

Figure 3.4. Current adjusting and flow balancing: a pseudokreisel with properly adjusted internal water current (A). The jellies are passing slowly upward along the left wall farthest from the outflow screen and dropping down through the viewing portal before being gently returned in the up-current. Notice that the jellies are not spinning around the entire perimeter of the tank, thus risking encounters with the outflow suction currents and screen. Stretch kreisel with currents properly adjusted (B). In this case, the jellies spend most of their time in the center of the tank, away from outflow screens.

● ●

Changes to current settings should be one of the first things you check when you suspect something is wrong with your jellies system. Oftentimes, decreasing the amount of water movement is the proper answer to flow problems.

● ●

A Step-by-Step Guide to Constructing a Simple Jellies System

1. Figure out what kind of jellyfish you want. For example, I would like to build a warm-water jelly tank in my garage for a school science project. The jellies are hardy and relatively easy to acquire online. And I don't need to use a kreisel because some of the warm-water jellyfish do not require

as carefully balanced currents to keep the jellies up and off the bottom of the tank.

2. Determine the care requirements for the target species (instructions are provided in chapter 7).

3. Learn how to acquire and maintain the food *Artemia* nauplii. Practice harvesting *Artemia* for a while before getting jellyfish. Good food leads to good health.

4. Collect the supplies. I like using a big cooler or an old display tank for a reservoir, a smaller tank for the jellies to be displayed in, a power head from the pet store to drive water through the system, metal halide lighting for the symbiotic algae living with the warm-water jellyfish (the most expensive component), aquarium-safe silicone, a recycled jug and some plastic army men as filter media for helpful bacteria to live on, a few common tools from your garage, some ½ inch PVC, and plastic tubing.

5. Make a trickle filter out of a recycled plastic bottle and some army men or plastic pirates, dinosaurs, or whatever you like (see appendix, fig. A4).

6. Assemble the modified box tank (see appendix, fig. A1).

7. Allow things to dry for at least twenty-four hours and then rinse the components with fresh wa-

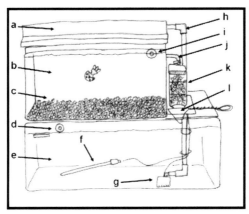

Figure 3.5. A simple jellyfish life-support system. I did not include a decorative outer case so the key components would be visible. The display tank is sitting on top of the reservoir, and inside the display tank are colored marbles for substrate. There is a polka-dotted lagoon jellyfish in the tank, which harbors symbiotic algae and requires full-spectrum lighting. The key components of this system are: metal halide lighting (A); exhibit tank (B); colored marbles as substrate (C); overflow-to-sewer drain (D); reservoir tank (E); heater (F); power head pump (G); water entering the display tank line (H); display-tank drain port (I); return-to-reservoir drain line (J); trickle filter (K); and bag filter (fine mesh net) (L).

ter. If you can, it is a good idea to presoak recently glued and cleaned PVC components in an already established system to "season" the newly constructed plumbing.

8. Connect the system. Plumb the pump to the tank, and add a display tank water flow control valve somewhere along the line where it is easily adjusted but out of view (don't forget aesthetics). Connect the outflow to the trickle filter.

••

After building the trickle filter, jelly tank, reservoir, and associated plumbing, it is a good idea to allow everything to dry well before adding water to the system. Once things are dry, rinse everything very well with fresh water. If possible, soak the components of the new system in a bathtub in order to rinse residual glue from the components. After that, you may wish to further soak components of your system in an established system in order to recruit helpful bacteria.

••

9. Start the pump to get the life-support system circulating. Plug in the heater, and normalize the temperature over several hours.

10. Once the system is normalized (e.g., proper current, temperature, salinity, etc.), add a test jellyfish to make sure the system is functional.

11. When the test jelly has survived with no deleterious effects for one to two hours, it is probably OK to add the remainder of the jellyfish collection to the display tank.

Further reading:

Greve, W. 1968. The "planktonkreisel," a new device for culturing zooplankton. *Marine Biology* 1(3):201–203.

Hamner, W. M. 1990. Design developments in the planktonkreisel, a plankton aquarium for ships at sea. *Journal of Plankton Research* 12(2):397–402.

Raskoff, K. A., F. A. Sommer, W. M. Hamner, and K. M. Cross. 2003. Collection and Culture Techniques for Gelatinous Zooplankton. *Biological Bulletin* 204:68–80.

3

JELLYFISH FOODS

Wild jellyfish eat zooplankton, which is usually made up of small aquatic animals. So it seems like a good idea to simply feed your captive jellies zooplankton. However, there aren't very many people I know who have daily access to fresh-caught zooplankton. So we jelly keepers need to feed our jellies appropriate substitutes. Finding nutritious foods for animals kept in aquaria is nothing new. Many aquarium foods have been developed over the years, and below I've described some appropriate foods for captive jellies.

Artemia nauplii (juvenile brine shrimp)

Most people are familiar with adult brine shrimp. They are readily available at pet stores. But as it turns out, adult brine shrimp aren't a very good food choice for most kinds of captive jellies. First, they aren't very nutritious, and second, jellies eat them but will only digest the insides of the brine shrimp and then spit out their shells. The shells end up sitting on the bottom of the tank and become sites for fouling organisms, or worse, they accumulate on the outflow screen and cause problems with currents in the tank.

Adult brine shrimp aren't a very good food for jellies, but their newly hatched juveniles are. A brine shrimp that has just hatched from its egg is called a nauplius, two or more are called nauplii (fig. 4.1A).

Artemia nauplii are a staple component of captive jellies' diets because the nauplii are small enough to be eaten, and they are relatively easy to obtain. *Artemia* nauplii usually arrive as cysts (kind of like eggs) in a can or a bag. I prefer to order *Artemia* nauplii shipped in a can rather than a vacuum sealed bag. My experience has been that canned cysts have higher hatch rates than nauplii that come in bags. My thinking is that some of the cysts in the vacuum-packed bags may get crushed during the packing process. When harvesting your nauplii, be very careful to remove as many cysts as possible before feeding the jellies. They can't digest the cysts, and if they do accidentally get them into their guts, the cysts eventually turn black and rot a hole through the bell.

For instructions on how to harvest and maintain *Artemia* nauplii, look online or see the *Plankton Culture Manual*, published by Florida Aqua Farms in 2001.

There is some debate among professional aquarists regarding the best method for removing the nauplii from their cysts. There are two popularly used methods. They are artificially decapsulating the nauplii from their cysts (basically melting the cysts away with bleach) or naturally hatching them in seawater. Both methods have pros and cons, and both methods are acceptable in my view.

If you choose to decapsulate the nauplii, less time is spent harvesting them because the decapsulation process is carried out in batches every two weeks or so. Daily feeding amounts are separated into small refrigerated containers, and when you are ready to feed, you simply add water and any enrichment media you choose. Another benefit with using decapsulated nauplii is there is less of a problem with tank-fouling hydroids, which means you may not have to bleach the tank as often in order to remove them. The downside of decapsulating nauplii is that the process involves using bleach to dissolve the cysts away from the nauplii, and the timed chemical reaction is stopped with another chemical, sodium thiosulfate. If you bleach the cysts for too long you can kill an entire batch of food, which is time and money wasted. It takes time to perfect your technique, and you also need a well-ventilated space in which to carry out the chemical reactions.

If you choose to hatch the nauplii naturally (my preferred method), no bleach is required. There is no risk of killing the nauplii by allowing the chemical reaction to go on too long. However, the nauplii do require daily water changes, and fouling hydroids seem to be more of a problem in tanks that are fed naturally hatched nauplii. I have always had great success when I fed jellyfish *Artemia* nauplii that were naturally hatched. Decapsulated *Artemia* nauplii have yielded mixed results for me, depending on whether it was a good batch or a bad batch. For that reason, I prefer to use the natural hatching method, which consistently performs well over time for me.

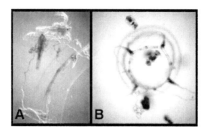

Figure 4.1. Appropriate captive jellyfish foods. Illustration (A) shows *Artemia* nauplii being stung and pulled in on the tentacles of a jelly. The nauplii are about 2mm long. Illustration (B) shows rotifers being stung and eaten by an immature cross jellyfish. The rotifers are about half a millimeter long.

Rotifers, *Brachionus* **sp.**

Rotifers are very small animals naturally present in marine and freshwater ecosystems (fig. 4.1B). They are smaller than *Artemia* nauplii, and they wander around eating things the size of bacteria. In fact, they are sometimes used in wastewater treatment plants to do just that. Compared to us, they have a very fast life cycle (something like two to eight days, depending on the species and gender). So it becomes important to do daily maintenance on your rotifer cultures if you plan to have them. If you only feed them once every two or three days, there may be entire generations of rotifers that you miss interacting with. I feed rotifers to animals with very small mouths, including early medusa stages of many jellies and jellyfish-producing hydroid cultures. For instructions on how to grow rotifers and where to get them please see the Florida Aqua Farms manual or look on the Internet.

Small Krill, *Euphausia pacifica*

When jellies are large, you can feed them small krill *(Euphausia pacifica)*. These are harvested from the wild and are a natural prey item for many different kinds of jellyfish.

Krill Shake

The idea here is to blend big, nutritious chunks of food into smaller, easier-to-eat chunks of food. Small krill and seawater are the principle ingredients, but you may also wish to include small pieces of different fish. I like using prawns (purchased from the grocery store), white bait smelt, and salmon. Add all of the ingredients to a blender and blend away! Use your imagination to make up your own shake concoctions. The seafood counter at the market should get your mind spinning. Try adding surf clams, mussels, and maybe even some crab meat into the mix. The bottom line is that many jellies will probably eat it. There is no set recipe.

> *Krill shake is a dangerous food item because it can clog the outflow cover screens!*

You need to be aware of consistency and texture when making krill shake. You don't want it to be a thick, gooey paste. A little runny is better than too thick. If the mixture is too thick, it can clog the screens on your system. When you make krill shake for the first few times, squirt a little of it into the sink, toilet, or somewhere there is water to ensure that the consistency is right (I do this every time I make up a new batch). It is good jelly-keeping practice to check the screens an hour or so after you feed out krill shake to make sure they aren't clogged. If you do acciden-tally foul the screens, brush them or siphon the debris right away. A good jelly aquarist will always brush the screens an hour or so after feeding out krill shake and again first thing in the morning the next day.

Moon Jellies, *Aurelia* sp.

In the wild, there is a jellyfish food chain with jellies higher on the chain eating jellies lower on the chain. Moon jellies are one of the easier kinds of jellyfish to grow and are a common prey of larger medusivorous jellyfish. Therefore, they are one of the most often used jellyfish as a captive jellyfish food. Feeding moon jellies to your medusivores will help keep the medusivores healthy, and they will be better able to regenerate lost parts.

Chopped Moon Jellies

This is exactly what it sounds like. Use a walnut chopper or something like it to chop moon jellies into smaller, easy-to-digest pieces. When raising the ephyrae of medusivorous jellies, smash some small moon jellies into a paste and feed out the resultant slurry to the medusivores.

Enrichments (Making Food Healthier)

When you feed one thing to an intended food organism in an effort to make the intended food item more nutritious, the process is referred to as bioencapsulation, or gut loading, and the end result is a more nutritious food item. By themselves, nauplii are not very nutritious. Luckily, enrichment media are available that can help make them more so. One option is to soak nauplii in Super Selco, which is an aquaculture product made up of many different good-for-your-jellyfish things (e.g., lipids, omega-3 fatty acids, and several vitamins). A little bit of Selco (self-emulsifying lipid concentrate) goes a long way. For very small-scale nauplii hatching operations, one small drop of Selco per liter of seawater should suffice. I know it is costly, but I assure you it makes a difference.

There is some debate among professional aquarists about whether the nauplii actually eat the Selco, or if they are just coated in it. When nauplii hatch from their cysts, they survive for about the first twenty-four hours on their yolk sacs alone. After about twenty-four hours, the nauplii molt to their second growth stage (they grow a bit) and develop their guts. Whether or not these nauplii are eating the Selco or are just soaked in it doesn't really matter. What matters is that jellies fed nauplii soaked in Selco grow larger and survive better in the early stages than jellies fed nauplii that have not been enriched with Selco.

As good as Selco is, you can't leave the nauplii soaking in it indefinitely. It coats their gills and will kill them if you leave them soaking in it for longer than thirty-six hours. Live *Artemia* nauplii are better for your jellyfish than dead ones. So soak nauplii in

Super Selco for one day and then rinse your nauplii using clean seawater and a fine mesh net the next day. After rinsing, return your nauplii to clean seawater and feed them some kind of phytoplankton on non-Selco enriching days. I use *Nannochloropsis* because it is relatively easy to obtain (you can purchase it as a paste from aquaculture supply vendors), and I find the light green color aesthetically appealing. Again, a little bit goes a long way: use about 2 mL of algae paste for 2 L of nauplii-containing seawater. The nauplii eat the algae and are more nutritious because they have a little something in their guts.

I also feed *Nannochloropsis* algae to my rotifers to make them more nutritious—this is a small-scale example of bioencapsulation. An extreme example of bioencapsulation would be feeding algae-enriched rotifers to your Super Selco–soaked *Artemia* nauplii and then feeding those nauplii to small moon jellyfish, which you then feed to a medusivore like the lion's mane jelly. Bioencapsulation is really all about food chains. Use your imagination, and I bet you can come up with your own dietary combinations that will work just as well or better than mine do.

Lighting

Some warm-water species of jellyfish harbor symbiotic algae called zooxanthellae similar to those found in corals and other animals. The association is mutually beneficial. The algae get a place to live, and waste from the algae feeds the jellies. Algae need light to make their energy. Therefore, full-spectrum lighting is a requirement for jellyfish harboring symbiotic algae. One can use the same lights one would use on a coral reef tank at home (e.g., compact fluorescents or metal halides, but old-fashioned actinics are not good enough) with all the same considerations one would use for corals (e.g., plan the lighting in accordance with the tank depth, etc.). A downside to lighted jellyfish aquariums is that diatoms quickly proliferate on the tank walls and windows, leading to routine cosmetic maintenance for the aquarist.

Key points about feeding:

1. *Don't feed the jellies food items that are larger than the jellies are themselves.* Feeding jellies things that are too large may kill the jellyfish. Or the jellies may attempt to eat the food item, but end up sinking to the bottom of the tank and becoming damaged.

2. *Don't overfeed the jellies.* Overfeeding may foul the water in your tank. Err on the side of underfeeding if you're unsure of how much food to add at the beginning, and slowly increase the feeding amount over time. You don't want uneaten food accumulating on the tank screens and walls because it can become substrate for fouling organisms.

3. *Be wary of screen-clogging foods.* If you make krill shake, be sure to check the outflow screens of the tank about one hour afterward. Too much debris in the water can clog the screens. The same could

be said if you feed out frozen "wild plankton" cubes. Dead foods cannot swim away from the screens and therefore tend to stick to them or sink to the bottom of the tank.

4. *Don't let nauplii sit in enrichment Selco water for longer than thirty-six hours.* The Selco coats the gills of the *Artemia* nauplii, decreasing survivor-ship over time. Enrich for one day, and then feed them out. Leftover nauplii should be rinsed with clean seawater and returned to their holding tank of clean seawater.

5. *Be wary of novel, shortcut foods.* There are no short-cuts in jelly husbandry. There are a few novel red-frozen-copepod concoctions out there that work great as food for fish but do not work as well for growing jellies. The red-frozen-copepods are attractive as food items because they appear to eliminate the need for time-consuming harvest-ing of *Artemia* nauplii. I respectfully submit that experience and my experiments have shown that red-frozen-copepods inhibit normal growth of some jellyfish species rather than enhance it.

6. *Be wary of frozen cube foods labeled "zooplankton."* Each batch is probably made up of a different variety of zooplankton. The composition of the plankton cubes depends on harvesting locations, methods of collection, and seasons. Look care-fully at the thawed plankton cubes to determine what is present before feeding them out to ensure

that no deleterious animals are included (like screen-clogging arrow worms or hole-in-the-jellyfish-bell-punching, spine-having porcelain crab zoea).

7. *Minimize the amount of residual cysts in the nauplii that are to be fed out!* The jellies will eat them but cannot digest them. The cysts instead rot holes in the bells of the jellies. To get as many of the cysts out as you can, perform a slow and careful nauplii separation. Take your time, have some coffee, and read the paper. Better yet, use harvesting time to talk with your kids or call your mom.

The Jelly Food Chain

In the wild, there is a jellyfish food chain. Jellyfish higher on the food chain eat jellies lower on the chain. The jellyfish food chain is important because many of the jellies we have in captivity eat other kinds of jellies. As it turns out, the jelly-like matrix making up the bell of one kind of jellyfish doesn't differ much chemically from other jellyfish. So it doesn't take very much energy for the predatory jellyfish to take apart the prey jelly's matrix and incorporate it into the predator's matrix. Therefore, breeding one kind of jelly to feed another may be a necessary kind of live-food culture effort, depending on the kind of jellyfish one wishes to keep. An example of a jellyfish hierarchy where jellies first on the list eat jellies below them would be as follows: egg yolk jelly (*Phacellophora camtschatica*), lion's mane jelly (*Cyanea* spp.), sea nettles (*Chrysaora* spp.), crystal jelly (*Aeqourea* spp.), moon jelly (*Aurelia* spp.)

Jellyfish as Food for People

There are many people in the world who like to eat jellyfish. Not all jellyfish are edible, but several kinds are. You can find edible jellyfish sold in packets at specialty markets and also online. A quick Internet search turns up several different recipes and methods for preparing jellyfish for human consumption. They are prepared and served in myriad ways. For example, jellyfish is listed as one of the ingredients in the seafood salad at my local grocery store (I have no idea which species). In my opinion, jellyfish alone haven't much flavor to them. When served as a meal, they taste like whatever sauce you prepare them in. Recently, I saw an article describing how the Japanese use them in jellyfish flavored ice cream.

4

ESSENTIAL JELLYFISH BIOLOGY

Basic Jellyfish Anatomy

MOST JELLYFISH HAVE similar body plans, which are simple when compared to other animals. The central portion of a jellyfish body is called the bell (fig. 5.1). Around the perimeter of the bell, at its margin, are tentacles that are loaded with stinging cells, which are also known as cnidocytes. Cnidocytes are the parent cells that generate the tiny darts called cnidae or nematocysts that jellyfish use to sting and inactivate their prey. It is from this term, cnida, that the phylum name for jellyfish and their cousins is derived, the phylum Cnidaria. Jellies don't have heads, and they don't have what zoologists call a complete gut (they have a mouth but no anus). Everything they eat is processed in a central bag-like stomach, where it is digested and distributed throughout the body in a series of canals. What isn't digested is egested right back out the mouth.

Jellyfish have sensory structures that allow them to monitor and react to their environments. Many can sense light, dark, and gravity. Some have been shown to detect food at a distance (using chemical detection, something akin to smell). They may even have escape responses to predation. For example, when a purple stripe jelly is approached in the field and given a sound thump on its side with a net, the jelly turns toward the bottom and increases its pulsing rate—in effect, a run response. It makes sense that if an ocean sunfish or a sea turtle takes a bite of the jellyfish, it turns toward the dark bottom water to escape and regenerate lost body parts. Just how much reacting to the environment jellyfish do remains to be seen, but don't be surprised to one day learn that they can be taught or conditioned to do something.

··
Jellyfish, corals, and sea anemones all poop out the same orifice they eat with.... So don't invite them to dinner because you may find their table manners lacking!
··

Stinging Cells

I feel like I would be shirking my duty here if I didn't say a few words about the stinging cells, how some of them work, and how to treat minor stings you may incur when jelly-keeping. There are a lot of different kinds of stinging cells, and they all have different functions, but the ones people are most concerned with are the ones that are designed to capture and inactivate prey. They tend to be the ones that cause the painful stinging, burning, and itching sensations people feel when they accidentally brush ex-

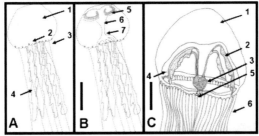

Figure 5.1. Illustrations (A) and (B) show basic anatomy of medusae belonging to the class Scyphozoa: 1. bell; 2. sensory structures; 3. tentacle; 4. oral arms; 5. gonads; 6. gut; 7. mouth (note that structures 5–7 are internal). Illustration (C) shows the basic anatomy of a medusa belonging to the class Hydrozoa: 1. bell; 2. gonads; 3. gut; 4. radial canal; 5. mouth; 6. tentacle. Scale bars = 10 cm and 2 cm in illustrations (B) and (C) respectively.

posed skin against the tentacles of a jelly. Tentacles, oral arms, and the outer surfaces of the jellyfish bell are all covered with stinging cells. Think of cnidae as tiny spring-loaded darts armed with neurotoxin.

The stinging cells themselves are basically made of a basement cell (the cnidocyte), a penetrating dart (the cnida), a cap, and a trigger. When something brushes against the trigger, the cap flies open and the dart springs out, attempting to penetrate and inject the neurotoxin (fig. 5.2). The neurotoxin slows the animal down or stops it, making it much easier to eat for the jellyfish because the prey struggles less.

Different kinds of jellies have different kinds of penetrating darts. Some have great big, long darts with strong neurotoxins. Jellies with those kinds of nematocysts probably eat things like fish and crustaceans in the wild. You need a big, strong dart to punch a hole through the shell of a swimming shrimp or krill, and you need powerful toxin to slow down a fish so it doesn't thrash around and tear up the jellies' bells. Other jellies have short darts that are designed for eating soft-bodied prey like invertebrate eggs and other kinds of jellyfish. Jellies with big darts hurt when they touch us, and jellies with small darts don't hurt because their darts can't get through our thick human skin. You may even be safe touching big-darted jellies if you touch them with calloused hands, but you could be in for a nasty surprise if you touch them with the inside of your forearm.

··

I don't mean to be crass here, but be sure to wash your hands after touching jellies or doing maintenance in their tanks. You don't want any unwelcome surprises the next time you use the restroom!

··

OK, so let's say you do get stung by the jellies in your care. What is it going to feel like? Really nasty stingers feel like someone is jamming a large gauge needle into your arm. But none of those species are covered in this book, and none of them are readily available in the aquarium trade. When you do get stung, it will most likely feel like a dull, burning sensation that may itch a little bit. Untreated, the stinging sensation will eventually stop, but you may get another little jab or two when you least suspect it if you don't remove any nematocysts that may still be present in the affected area. You may get a surprise the next time you hop in the shower as more unfired stinging cells are triggered. Warm water also awakens the itching sensation. You may wake up in the middle of the night itching and wanting to scratch the stung area. Don't scratch, however, because you

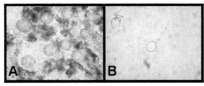

Figure 5.2. Illustration (A) shows unfired nematocysts, while (B) shows discharged nematocysts.

could scratch away your skin and cause an infection. Treat the stings when they occur.

Here are the methods I use to treat jelly stings. I am not a physician, but these are methods that I feel work pretty well. Also, it is important to realize there is no one simple remedy that cures all jellyfish stings because there are many different kinds of jellies, and not all of them carry the same toxins. Once you're stung, those darts have been fired into your skin and their neurotoxins released—that's why it hurts, it's physical and chemical trauma on a small scale.

I try to deactivate the stingers by pouring vinegar over the affected area. If you are on a picnic, you can spread mustard on the sting because mustard is full of vinegar. Some folks prescribe urinating on the sting to deactivate the stingers, but personally, I would use vinegar first and urine only as a last resort. Other folks like to use rubbing alcohol. I had the opportunity to be on the television show *Mythbusters* once, and we tested the effectiveness of pouring vodka on stung areas. It actually worked for nullifying the effects of a Pacific sea nettle sting. But be aware that we didn't test it on all of the species in my care at the time.

After pouring something on the area to deactivate nematocysts, it is important to remove any unfired darts that may be still present on your skin. I like to rinse the affected area with salt water and use a soft brush to gently brush the darts off my skin. Gently pat dry the area, or let it air dry, and then apply a topical antihistamine cream. That should do it. If you start feeling light-headed, have a rapid pulse, and feel nauseous and weak coupled with rapid breathing, consult a physician—quickly.

Part 2
Jelly Keeping

5

JELLYFISH ACQUISITION

Where the Wild Ones Live

MOST WILD JELLYFISH occur in marine environments, although there are some freshwater varieties, so two popular methods for collecting jellyfish are dock walking and boating. When a collector goes dock walking, he or she usually carries a long-handled dip net and a bucket. They also bring along a few collecting bags, one for each species. Dock walking is a lot of fun because you always see something different, but stay alert, be careful, and remain aware of your surroundings at all times. You don't want to surprise a sleeping sea lion, and you don't want to bonk your head on the bow of a fishing vessel!

I only recommend boating to collect jellies if you are a qualified and skilled boater or can get a licensed captain to handle boat operations safely. An ideal boating day for collecting jellyfish is one where the sea is flat and calm, with only a very slight breeze.

In Monterey Bay, it is generally better to go collecting first thing in the morning because conditions for jelly hunting tend to deteriorate as the day progresses and the wind picks up. Also, many jellies are vertical migrators, spending the night at the surface and heading for deeper water when the sun rises. The best places to look for jellies are on the edges of the glassy slicks on the surface of the water. The slicks are the result of wind gently blowing on the surface waters.

Internet Providers and More

There always seem to be a few people actively growing jellyfish in their garage laboratories, and there are usually a few commercial collectors, too. You can find them with a quick web search. Look up "moon jellies for sale" or something like that. Still, when compared to the fish keepers, there aren't that many people culturing jellyfish for sale these days. And there are more people wanting jellies than there are suppliers. Jellies for sale online are often listed as "not available at this time." A second reason jellies aren't always available is that wild ones tend to appear seasonally and episodically. Those who collect and sell jellies from the field are only able to get them at certain times of the year and only as weather permits. So when the wild-caught jellies are gone, you have to wait until next season to get more if you don't have cultures going.

How to Ship Jellyfish

Shipping jellyfish is certainly possible given the right equipment, care, and time. The primary issues involved with shipping jellyfish are increasing temperatures in the shipping boxes and deteriorating water quality conditions in the shipping bags. First, ensure that you are being responsible in your jellyfish shipping. Be sure to follow all laws and regulations pertaining to live-animal shipping, particularly when dealing with international colleagues. Also, kindly remind colleagues not to spread non-native species where they don't belong. Responsible deacquisition of your jellies is imperative.

I prefer to ship jellyfish in the recycled, large cooler boxes originally used to ship fish. You can obtain them at the local pet store, or you can make your own by cutting up old Styrofoam and taping it together with packing tape. The shipping guys don't like packages that leak, and airplane pilots get really nervous about the idea of salt water dripping into their airplane electronics at forty thousand feet, so I tend to overbag my seawater—I double-bag everything.

Don't feed the jellyfish for at least twenty-four hours before shipping them. Jellies getting sloshed around during shipping tend to egest any materials in their guts, leaving an orange, slime-coated goo (jellyfish puke) in the shipping bag. This can lead to poor water quality and unhappy jellyfish. To avoid the unhappiness of jellyfish puke in the shipping bags, don't feed the jellies prior to the event. Missing a meal or two won't kill them in the short term.

To ship the jellies, first place two large, square-bottomed bags inside the cooler box. The bags with jellyfish in them will rest inside the two larger bags (we will be double-bagging the double-bagged jellyfish). Fill a small, square-bottomed collection bag with 2L–3L of water, then gently add a jellyfish or two to the bag. Next, squeeze all of the air out of the jellyfish bag and twist the top closed and rubber band it. Put the bag inside another bag and rubber band it shut , then place them into the larger shipping box. I tend to ship four to six bags of water at a time. Shipping more water is costly, but is better in terms of water quality for the animals. Don't skimp on water-shipping costs.

••

You can pack many small moon jellies together in a single bag, but sea nettles and crystal jellies should be bagged as single animals. Too many sea nettles together foul the water, and crystal jellies can be cannibalistic.

••

If the jellyfish come from temperate zones and need to stay cool on their journey, I add one or two cold packs inside the shipping box between bags with jellies in them. These will serve for a day or two. If the jellyfish are tropical ones, heat packs can be used. When all the bags and temperature packs are in place, close and rubber band the large retaining bags inside the cooler box. Next, fill the space between the top of the closed bags and the cooler box lid with packing peanuts, which are great insulators. Then write a nice note to the people who are receiving the jellies with any special instructions or a thank-you for purchasing them. Then tape the box closed, weigh it, and head off to the shipping shop. You absolutely should send them for overnight delivery.

After you have received your new jellies, it is courteous to let the supplier know they arrived and in what condition. Remove the jellies from their cooler box and float/suspend them in their intended tank for ten to fifteen minutes. Slowly add a little tank water into the bag and watch for adverse effects (retracted tentacles, ceased swimming). If nothing bad happens, add a few jellyfish to your tank and watch them for thiry minutes. If everything is stable, go ahead and add the rest of the bagged jellyfish to the tank. Wait at least twelve hours before you feed them to ensure that you have properly adjusted currents without the confounding variable of retracted tentacles.

6

CARE INSTRUCTIONS BY SPECIES

NOT ALL JELLYFISH that can be cultured turn out to be good display animals. Some of them are too small to see, and they often get caught in the screens. Other kinds of jellies have dietary requirements that are too difficult to meet. A good candidate for a displayable jellyfish is one that is tough, possesses charisma, has longevity, and is easy to acquire. Also consider the cost of feeding them both in terms of time, maintenance, space, and finances.

It's also important to choose appropriate species for display and culture. For example, there are at least sixteen different kinds of moon jellies known so far. *Aurelia aurita* moon jellies have polyps that are easy to cause to strobilate, but *A. labiata* moon jellies have polyps that are difficult to cause to strobilate. However, *A. labiata* moon jellies grow larger, and I feel they are more attractive than the *A. aurita*, so the additional work is worth it for me in producing *A. labiata*. The following descriptions for maintaining specific species of jellyfish are given in order from easiest to hardest. Another way of saying it is that moon jellies are the easiest to grow of the given species, while lobed comb jellies are the most challenging.

Moon Jellies (*Aurelia* sp.)

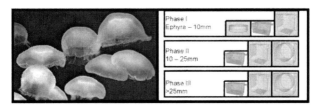

Figure 7.1. *Left*, moon jellies *(Aurelia aurita)* about 20 cm in bell diameter. *Right*, tanks for growing moon jellies. Phase I, eight-inch diameter culture dish without stirrer or screened-in flow-through tank, one- or two-foot diameter pseudokreisel. Phase II, screened-in flow-through tank, one- or two-foot diameter pseudokreisel, four- or five-foot diameter round kreisel. Phase III, modified box tanks, two-foot diameter pseudokreisel, four- or five-foot round kreisel

- *Description*: Wild medusae of *A. labiata* range in color from translucent purple to pinkish-peach. Small medusae (< 5 cm in diameter) are more translucent. Captive, older specimens turn brownish when their health starts to deteriorate. Moon jellies have short frilly mouth arms, and the bell margin is ringed with short slender tentacles.

- *Distribution/Range*: Scattered globally. Depending on your source, up to sixteen cryptic *Aurelia* species are known. To distinguish some species, molecular tools must be used. *Aurelia labiata* is the local moon jelly in Monterey Bay, California.

- *General remarks*: *Aurelia* medusae feed on zooplankton and are in turn fed upon by some fish, sea turtles, and other jellyfish. They host parasitic amphipods, medusae fish, and butterfish. Medusae and polyps are relatively easy to acquire and do comparatively well in captive environments, making moons one of the most commonly displayed jellyfish at zoos and aquariums.

Different species of *Aurelia* have different cues inducing their polyps to strobilate. *Aurelia aurita* polyps held at 15°C will produce strobilae unassisted in episodic waves every two to four months. If you're in a hurry to produce ephyrae, try turning off the incoming tank water and adding three to five drops of Lugol's solution (iodine seems to be the key ingredient) to the polyp culture. Allow the polyps to soak for one or two days, and then return the flow. You may also want to try giving the polyp culture a good cleaning. Sometimes the small amount of disturbance stress kicks them into gear. Another useful and good method is to drop the tank temperature to 10°C for two to three weeks and then return the temperature to 14°C–15°C. Strobilae should form in two to three weeks.

Water quality/environment:

Temperature: 12ºC–21ºC.
Salinity: 28–34 ppt

- *Rearing Instructions*: Phase I medusae are newly released ones that range up to 10 mm in bell diameter. They do well in dishes with standing seawater given daily water changes, screened-in flow-through tanks, and one- or two-foot tall pseudokreisels.

  Phase II medusae measuring from 10–25 mm in diameter do well in screened-in flow-through tanks, pseudokreisels, and four-foot-tall round kreisels.

Phase III medusae, jellies larger than 25 mm in diameter similarly do well in screened-in flow-through tanks, pseudokreisels, and kreisels. Move them to a four- or five-foot kreisel when medusae are about 30 mm in diameter. If tank currents are properly adjusted, moon jellies fare well in just about all types of jellyfish tanks.

Table 7.1 Suggested diet for cultured moon jellies (*Aurelia* sp.)

Life history stage	Food type	Feeding frequency	Recommended amount
Large medusae (Phase III) > 25 mm	Artemia nauplii Small krill Blended salmon Krill shake Wild plankton	Daily 2–3x per week 1x per week 1x per week As available	250–350 mL 3–5 pieces per animal 1 baster 1 baster Whatever you have
Small medusae (Phase II) 10–25 mm	Artemia nauplii Rotifers	Daily Daily	150 mL 100 mL
Ephyrae (Phase I) Ephyra–10 mm	Artemia nauplii Rotifers	Daily Daily	25 mL 25 mL
Polyps	Artemia nauplii	Daily	50 mL

Further reading:

Albert, D. J. 2005. Reproduction and longevity of *Aurelia labiata* in Roscoe Bay, a small bay on the Pacific coast of Canada. *Journal of the Marine Biological Association of the United Kingdom* 85:575–581.

Arai, M. N. 1991. Attraction of *Aurelia* and *Aequorea* to prey. *Hydrobiologia* 216–217:363–366.

Behrends, G., and Schneider, G. 1995. Impact of *Aurelia aurita* medusae (Cnidaria, Scyphozoa) on the standing stock and community composition of mesozooplankton in the Kiel Bight (western Baltic Sea) *Marine ecology progress series*. 127 (1–3): 39–45.

Caughlan, D. 1984. The captive husbandry of *Aurelia aurita*. *Drum and Croaker* 21(1).

Hamner, W. M., and R. M. Jenssen. 1974. Growth, Degrowth, and Irreversible Cell Differentiation in *Aurelia aurita*. *American Zoologist* 14(2):833–849.

Lucas, C. H. 2001. Reproduction and life history strategies of the common jellyfish, *Aurelia aurita*, in relation to its ambient environment. *Hydrobiologia* 451:229–246.

Miyake, H., M. Terazaki, and Y. Kakinuma 2002. On the polyps of the common jellyfish *Aurelia au-*

rita in Kagoshima Bay. *Journal of Oceanography* 58(3):451–459.

Purcell, J. E. 2000. Aggregations of the jellyfish *Aurelia labiata*: abundance, distribution, association with age-0 walleye pollock, and behaviors promoting aggregation in Prince William Sound, Alaska, USA. *Marine Ecology Progress Series* 195:145–158.

Purcell, J. E. 2007. Environmental effects on asexual reproduction rates of the scyphozoan *Aurelia labiata*. *Marine Ecology Progress Series* 348:183–196.

Widmer, C. L. 2005. Effects of temperature on growth of Northeast Pacific moon jellyfish ephyrae, *Aurelia labiata* (Cnidaria: Scyphozoa). *Journal of the Marine Biological Association of the United Kingdom* 85:569–573.

Upside-down Jellies (*Cassiopeia* sp.)

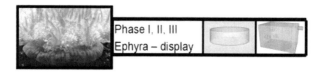

Figure 7.2. *Left,* upside-down jelly (*Cassiopeia* sp.). *Right,* rearing vessels for upside-down jellies. Phase I, eight-inch diameter culture dish without a stirrer. Phases II and III, all kinds of modified boxes (many possibilities).

- *Description*: These striped jellies have a flattened bell with curled edges and several mouth arms. They are olive drab green to blue in color, depending on the species. Some are better looking than others. They are called upside-down jellies because they are normally oriented with the bell exumbrella pointing downward and oral arms pointing skyward.
- *Distribution/Range*: Subtropics to tropics, circumglobal, Caribbean, Hawaii, southern Florida
- *General remarks*: Upside-down jellies live in tropical to subtropical salt marsh lagoon flats and lay on their exumbrellae with oral arms pointed toward the sun. They harbor symbiotic zooxanthellae, which give them their golden brown color. I lived in the Florida Keys for a few years, and when I used to go wading through the salt flats, carpets of *Cassiopeia* somehow sensed I was there and would emit strands of nematocyst-laden mucus for me to wade into. It was an effective mechanism for making me want to avoid them.

These jellyfish are relatively bomb-proof in my opinion. They are very hardy and tolerant to a wide range of environmental conditions. Upside-down jellies are a good place to start for the new jelly aquarist wanting a measure of success on the first go around. The only downside to these jellies is that they don't get up off the bottom to swim around very often, which may not be to an individual aquarist's liking. If seeing jellies swimming around the middle of the tank is not an issue for you, and you want a good, tough breed of jellyfish to start with, try these.

••
It is cheaper and easier to heat water than it is to chill it.
••

I have gone on vacation for extended periods and not fed them for as long ten days (I did, however, keep the full spectrum lighting on its twelve on/twelve off cycle). They have been able to survive nicely on light alone for those short durations.

Water quality/environment:

Temperature: 18ºC–25ºC
Salinity: 33 ppt, but tolerant to wide fluctuations.
Light levels: Thrive with full-spectrum lighting.

•   *Rearing Instructions*: Phase I, II, and III medusae all do well in modified box-style tanks. They do poorly in kreisels.

Polyps should be kept in isolated culture tanks.

They strobilate on their own and require very
little care, relatively speaking. In the mangrove
lagoons in the Florida Keys, the polyps naturally
occur on fallen, submerged mangrove leaves. Living in rapidly changing mangrove lagoon environments requires that polyps be highly tolerant
to fluctuating environmental conditions. It also
requires that the polyps are able to generate new
medusae quickly, which they are. Ephyrae should
be fed Artemia nauplii, kept in 8-inch dishes or
ephyra catch tanks and exposed to daylight full
spectrum lighting (twelve hours on and twelve
hours off).

Cassiopeia are hardy animals, making them
good at being fouling organisms. They are prime
candidate for accidental introduction as a non-
native species in places where they don't belong.
They are very prolific, and you will shortly find
polyps in the reservoir and any other system that
is connected to that reservoir (danger!). In my
professional experience, we didn't need to keep
polyps in culture. The exhibit and reservoir produced enough polyps and plenty of ephyrae without our meddling.

· *Species compatibility*: They may be held together
with the spotted lagoon jelly (*Mastigias* sp.),
which makes for a nice display because the upside-down jellies lay on the bottom of the tank,
forming a carpet of jellies, while the spotted lagoon jellies occupy the midwater.

Table 7.2. Suggested diet for cultured upside-down jellies.

Life history stage	Food type	Feeding frequency	Recommended amount
Large medusae (Phase III) > 25 mm	Artemia nauplii	Daily, use an autofeeder set to feed out 3–5 times per day	500–1000 mL
	Full-spectrum lighting	Daily	12 hours on/12 hours off
	Wild plankton	As available	Whatever you have
Small medusae (Phase II) 10–25 mm	Artemia nauplii	Daily	300 mL
	Full spectrum lighting	Daily	12 hours on/12 hours off
Ephyrae (Phase I) Ephyra–10 mm	Artemia nauplii	Daily	25 mL
	Full spectrum lighting	Daily	12 hours on/12 hours off
Polyps	Artemia nauplii	Daily	50 mL

Further reading:

Colley, N. J., and R. K. Trench. 1983. Selectivity in phagocytosis and persistence of symbiotic algae by the scyphistoma stage of the jellyfish *Cassiopeia xamachana*. *Proceedings of the Royal Society of London* 219:61–82.

Fitt, K. W. 1984. The role of chemosensory behavior of *Symbiodinium microadriaticum*, intermediate hosts, and host behavior in the infection of coelenterates and molluscs with zooxanthellae. *Marine Biology* 81(1):9–17.

Pierce, J. 2005. A system for mass culture of upside-down jellyfish *Cassiopeia* spp. as a potential food item for medusivores in captivity. *International Zoo Yearbook* 39(1):62–69.

Rahat, M., and O. Adar. 1980. Effect of symbiotic zooxanthellae and temperature on budding and strobilation in *Cassiopeia andromeda* (Eschscholz). *Biological Bulletin* 159(2):394–401.

Verdelr, E. A., and L. R. McCloskey. 1998. Production, respiration, and photophysiology of the mangrove jellyfish Cassiopea xamachana symbiotic with zooxanthellae: effect of jellyfish size and season. Marine Ecology Progress Series 168:147–162.

Spotted Lagoon Jelly (Mastigias papua)

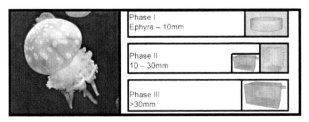

Figure 7.3. *Left*, the spotted lagoon jelly (*Mastigias papua*). *Right*, tanks for growing medusae of *Mastigias*. Phase I, eight-inch diameter culture dish without a stirrer. Phase II, screened-in flow-through tank or a one-foot diameter pseudokreisel. Phase III, modified box tanks (all kinds of possibilities).

- *Description*: Golden brown to blue in color, very actively pulsing jellies with large white spots reminiscent of a large mushroom. The "cap" of the mushroom is really the jelly's bell, and trailing from under the bell are the mouth arms, each covered with hundreds of microscopic mouths.
- *Distribution/range*: Palau saltwater lagoons, South Pacific
- *General remarks*: These active jellies swim throughout the water column and don't rely on incoming water currents to keep them off the bottom of the tank. They harbor symbiotic zooxanthellae, which require full spectrum lighting. The lighting timer should be set to turn on for twelve hours and off for twelve hours. One should also use a timed autofeeder with the autofeeder set to feed at 8-hour intervals.

Without food, they sit on the bottom of the

tank and pulse slowly. They may be tending their symbiotic algae by turning their bell down and presenting the algae upward, toward the light. When food is introduced to the tank, the jellies change modes and begin swimming around the tank and hunting for food. When all the food is gone they return to the bottom and resume the business of algae farming.

These jellies grow really fast. They can double their size in a month, but still do well in relatively small aquariums (15–20 gallon modified box tank).

The medusae are relatively easy to acquire and maintain. They are tough, good looking, and active, making them one of my favorite jellies in small systems.

Water quality/environment:

Temperature: 20ºC–25ºC
Salinity: 33 ppt

- *Rearing instructions*: Phase I medusae are ones that have just released from their parent strobila to about 10 mm in bell diameter. The ephyrae may be maintained in a standing dish of seawater and given daily water changes or placed in a one-foot diameter pseudokreisel. Include full-spectrum lighting (twelve hours on/twelve hours off) and feed them *Artemia* nauplii daily.

    Phase II medusae are ones measuring from 10–30 mm in bell diameter. They may be kept in all kinds of tank designs, but they don't do very well in standard kreisels. They are able to keep themselves suspended off the tank bottom so they do not require the currents generated by a kreisel tank and therefore do better in modified box-style tanks. Include full spectrum lighting (twelve hours on/twelve hours off) and feed them *Artemia* nauplii daily.

Phase III medusae are ones with bell diameters measuring 30 mm or larger. They are best kept in modified box-style tanks. Include full-spectrum lighting (twelve hours on/twelve hours off) and feed them *Artemia* nauplii daily.

- *Species compatibility*: They may be maintained together with the upside-down jelly (*Cassiopeia* sp.).

Table 7.3. Suggested diet for cultured spotted lagoon jellies (*Mastigias* sp.)

Life history stage	Food type	Feeding frequency	Recommended amount
Large medusae (Phase III) > 30mm	Artemia nauplii	Daily	500–1000 mL
	Krill shake	1x per week	150 mL per tank
	Wild plankton	As available	Whatever you have
	Full-spectrum lighting	Daily	12 hours on/12 hours off
	Fish eggs	As available	
Small medusae (Phase II) 10–30 mm	Artemia nauplii	Daily	300 mL
	Rotifers	Daily	100 mL
	Full spectrum lighting	Daily	12 hours on/12 hours off
Ephyrae (Phase I) Ephyra–10 mm	Artemia nauplii	Daily	25 mL
	Rotifers	Daily	25 mL
	Full spectrum lighting	Daily	12 hours on/12 hours off
Polyps	Artemia nauplii	Daily	25 mL
	Rotifers	Daily	25 mL

Further reading:

Dawson, M. N. 2005. Morphological variation and systematics in the Scyphozoa: *Mastigias* (Rhizostomeae, Mastigiidae)—a golden unstandard? *Hydrobiologia* 537(1–3):185–206.

Dawson, M. N., and W. M. Hamner. 2003. Geographic variation and behavioral evolution in marine plankton: the case of *Mastigias* (Scyphozoa, Rhizostomeae). *Marine Biology* 143:1161–1174.

Hamner, W., and I. R. Hauri. 1981. Long-distance horizontal migrations of zooplankton (Scyphomedusae: *Mastigias*). *Limnology and Oceanography* 26(3):414–423.

McCloskey, L. R., L. Muscatine, and F. P. Wikerson. 1994. Daily photosynthesis, respiration, and carbon budgets in a tropical marine jellyfish (*Mastigias* sp.). *Marine Biology* 119(1):13–22.

Sugiura, Y. 1965. On the life-history of rhizostome medusae III. On the effects of temperature on the strobilation of *Mastigias papua*. *Biological Bulletin* 128:493–496.

Lion's Mane Jelly (*Cyanea* sp.)

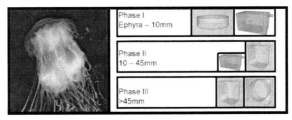

Figure 7.4. *Left,* lion's mane jelly (*Cyanea capillata*). *Right,*
tanks for growing medusae of *Cyanea.* Phase I, eight-inch
diameter culture dish without stirrer or screened-in flow-
through tank. Phase II, screened-in flow-through tank, one- or
two-foot diameter pseudokreisel. Phase III, two-foot diameter
pseudokreisel, four- or five-foot diameter round kreisel.

- *Description*: The commonly cultured lion's mane
  jelly (*Cyanea capillata*) has an orange bell with
  long, trailing, thin tentacles that when extended
  are white in color. Gulf of Mexico specimens are
  brownish in color with stripes radiating from a
  central ring to the edges of the bell.
- *Distribution/range*: Scattered distribution globally, several known species.

  ••
  To keep jelly tentacles from sticking to
  wooden poles or net handles, cover the
  handles with plastic tubing. Jelly tentacles
  usually don't stick to plastic.
  ••

- *General remarks*: There appear to be a number of
  different species of jellyfish that are all referred to
  as *Cyanea capillata.* Ones in the Arctic can grow
  up to three meters across, but the ones from the
  Gulf of Mexico and Chesapeake Bay don't get
  much bigger than a basketball. I suspect that very
  soon, someone using molecular tools will show

they are all truly different species, and they will all get new scientific names. *Cyanea* are medusivores and predators of zooplankton. In a fight between the medisivore titans *Cyanea* and *Phacellophora,* the *Phacellophora* wins.

It is a good practice to feed moon jellyfish about a half hour to forty-five minutes before wiping down the insides of the display tank. That way you avoid tangling and losing tentacles that accidentally stick to the cleaning pole. Older specimens in captivity begin losing their tentacles before perishing.

If you overstock the tank the jellies will become tangled.

Water quality/environment:
Temperature: 6°C–15°C
Salinity: 34 ppt

- *Rearing instructions*: Phase I consists of newly released ephyrae up to 10 mm in bell diameter. They do well in dishes with standing seawater that are given daily water changes, and they also do OK in screened-in flow-through tanks. Feed the jellies *Artemia* nauplii, rotifers, and smashed moon jellies daily.

  Phase II medusae measure from 10–45 mm in diameter and do well in screened-in flow-through tanks and one- and two-foot diameter pseudokreisels. Feed the jellies *Artemia* nauplii, rotifers- and diced moon jellies daily.

  Phase III medusae are larger than 45 mm in diameter and do well in two-foot diameter pseudokreisels and four- and five-foot diameter kreisels. Feed the jellies *Artemia* nauplii, rotifers, and *Aurelia* ephyrae daily.

- *Species compatibility*: You can mix *Cyanea capillata* with *C. versicolor* with no ill effects. If you mix them with egg yolk jellies (*Phacellophora camtschatica*), the lion's mane jellies get eaten. If you mix them with the siphonophore *Praya* (a relative of the Portuguese man-o-war) a horrible war ensues. Both animals take beatings and lose tentacles, but eventually they both coexist after each has run out of tentacles to fight with. This tentacle loss ultimately leads to the demise of both species because both lose the ability to catch food. A lesson is learned from this Pyrrhic truce.

Table 7.4. Suggested diet for cultured lion's mane jellies.

Life history stage	Food type	Feeding frequency	Recommended amount
Large medusae (Phase III) > 45 mm	*Artemia* nauplii	Daily	350–500 mL
	Small krill	2–3x per week	3–5 pieces per animal
	Small or chopped moon jellies	Daily	2–3 small moons each
	Wild plankton	As available	Whatever you have
Small medusae (Phase II) 10–45 mm	*Artemia* nauplii	Daily	150 mL
	Rotifers	Daily	100 mL
	Diced moon jellies	Daily	1 pipette
Ephyrae (Phase I) Ephyra–10 mm	*Artemia* nauplii	Daily	25 mL
	Rotifers	Daily	25 mL
	Diced moon jellies	Daily	1 pipette
Polyps	*Artemia* nauplii	Daily	25 mL
	Rotifers	Daily	25 mL

Further reading:

Bamstedt, U., M. B. Martinussen, and S. Matsakis. 1994. Trophodynamics of the two scyphozoan jellyfishes, *Aurelia aurita* and *Cyanea capillata*, in western Norway. *ICES Journal of Marine Science* 51(4):369–382.

Heeger, T., H. Moller, and U. Mrowietz. 1992. Protection of human skin against jellyfish (*Cyanea capillata*) stings. *Marine Biology* 113(4):669–678.

Lynam, C. P., S. J. Hay, and A. S. Brierley. 2005. Jellyfish abundance and climatic variation: contrasting responses in oceanographically distinct regions of the North Sea, and possible implications for fisheries. *Journal of the Marine Biological Association of the United Kingdom* 85:435–450.

Purcell, J. E. 2003. Predation on zooplankton by large jellyfish, *Aurelia labiata, Cyanea capillata* and *Aequorea aequorea*, in Prince William Sound, Alaska. *Marine Ecology Progress Series* 246:137–152.

Titelman, J., L. Gandon, A. Goarant, and T. Nilsen. 2007. Intraguild predatory interactions between the jellyfish *Cyanea capillata* and *Aurelia aurita*. *Marine Biology* 152(4):745–756.

Sea Gooseberry (*Pleurobrachia* sp.)

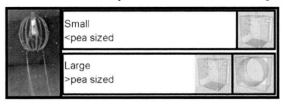

Figure 7.5. *Left,* sea gooseberry (*Pleurobrachia bacheii*). *Right,* tanks for keeping sea gooseberries. Small ones do well in a one-foot diameter pseudokreisel. Ones larger than a pea do well in two-foot diameter pseudokreisels and four- to five-foot diameter round kreisels.

- *Description*: Sea gooseberries are smallish, transparent, oval-shaped comb jellies. They propel themselves through the water using eight ciliated comb rows equidistant around the external perimeter of the body. When white light is shown upon the ciliated comb rows, the light is diffracted, resulting in rainbow—a really neat display effect.
- *Distribution/range*: Bering Sea to southern California.
- *General remarks*: They are usually present in Monterey Bay during the spring, although sometimes they are present year round. Small ones may be found by the careful eye in plankton tows. Interestingly, they are often found in the same plankton collections as the bell jelly, (*Eutonina indicans*).

    While fishing for zooplankton, sea gooseberries cast a net with two finely branched tentacles. As prey are captured, the sea gooseberry spins round and round passing its food laden tentacles across the mouth and lips. They are in turn preyed upon by other comb jellies and often parasitized by small amphipods.

The tentacles of comb jellies are loaded with sticking cells, not stinging cells. Comb jellies belong to the phylum Ctenophora, which translates to "comb bearers," and are a bit more structurally complex than jellyfish. They possess the evolutionary beginnings of a head end and a back end, and there are several other differences. But the important thing to note here is that they don't sting their prey like jellyfish do (which belong to the phlyum Cnidaria), meaning there is no danger of ever being stung by a comb jelly.

Water quality/environment:

Temperature: 7ºC–15ºC
Salinity: 34 ppt

- *Rearing instructions*: They grow quickly in one-foot diameter pseudokreisels. Move them up to two-foot diameter pseudokreisels when they are a bit larger than a pea. Ones larger than a pea can also be kept in four-foot diameter round kreisels. Feed them *Artemia* nauplii daily.
- *Species compatibility*: They may be kept with the bell jelly, *Eutonina indicans*. Interestingly, they are often collected together in the same plankton tows.

Table 7.5. Suggested laboratory diet for sea
gooseberries (*Pleurobrachia* sp.)

Life history stage	Food type	Feeding frequency	Recommended amount
All stages	*Artemia* nauplii	Daily	350–500 mL

Further reading:

Esserl, M., W. Greve, and M. Boersma. 2004. Effects of temperature and the presence of benthic predators on the vertical distribution of the ctenophore *Pleurobrachia pileus*. *Marine Biology* 145(3):595–601.

Gibbons, M. J., and S. J. Painting. 1992. The effects and implications of container volume on clearance rates of the ambush entangling predator *Pleurobrachia pileus* (Ctenophora: Tentaculata). *Journal of Experimental Marine Biology and Ecology* 163(2):199–208.

Greene, C. H., M. R. Landry, and B. C. Monger. 1986. Foraging behavior and prey selection by the ambush entangling predator *Pleurobrachia bachei*. *Ecology* 67(6):1493–1501.

Mutlu, E., and F. Bingel. 1999. Distribution and abundance of ctenophores, and their zooplankton food in the Black Sea. I. *Pleurobrachia pileus*. *Marine Biology* 135(4):589–601.

Yip, S. Y. 1984. Parasites of *Pleurobrachia pileus* Müller, 1776 (Ctenophora), from Galway Bay, western Ireland. *Journal of Plankton Research* 6(1):107–121.

Bell Jelly (*Eutonina indicans*)

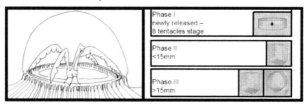

Figure 7.6. *Left*, the bell jelly (*Eutonina indicans*). *Right*, tanks for growing medusae of *Eutonina indicans*. Phase I, eight-inch diameter culture dish with a stirrer. Phase II, one-foot diameter pseudokreisel. Phase III, two-foot diameter pseudokreisel, four- or five-foot diameter round kreisel

- *Description*: They have a transparent, dome-shaped bell that is taller than it is wide. The gonads are visible as four wavy white stripes running down the lengths of the gut canals.
- *Distribution/range*: Bering Sea to southern California.
- *General remarks*: In Monterey Bay, they are generally present at the surface during spring but may also be present year-round. They occasionally host larval slender crabs and their gonads are parasitized by the small sea anemone, (*Peachia*) (fig. 11.4.c).

••

Use caution when cleaning display tank windows. Excessively contacting these jellies with tools during maintenance will cause them to perish.

••

Eutonina indicans are nice little hydrozoan jellies that are relatively easy to maintain. These bell jellies spawn after exposure to light following ten to twelve hours of darkness. They grow quickly but have relatively short lifespans in captivity. Displayable medusae, ones about 20mm in bell diameter, may be produced in about eight to ten weeks. They continue to grow and reach sexual maturity on display.

Water quality/environment:

Temperature: 7ºC–15ºC
Salinity: 33 ppt
Light levels: Probably prefer lower levels of light.

- *Rearing instructions*: Phase I consists of newly released medusae up to the early eight tentacles stage. They do well in both dishes with standing or stirred seawater using a plus-shaped magnetic stir bar and given daily water changes. They may also grow in a screened-in flow-through tank, but the success rate may not be as high without carefully balanced tank currents. Feed them rotifers only for the first two weeks. After that, feed them a small amount of *Artemia* nauplii mixed with rotifers.

  Phase II medusae, those having eight to thirty-two tentacles, do well in one-foot diameter pseudokreisels. Feed them *Artemia* nauplii daily.

  Phase III medusae, ones with more than thirty-two tentacles, do well in two-foot diameter pseudokreisels and four- and five-foot diameter round kreisels.

- *The hydroid:* Hydroids should be maintained in standing seawater, resting in temperature-controlled baths at 14°C. Feed them a small amount of rotifers every other day, and give the cultures gentle water changes each day. Water changes should be carefully done by flushing the cultures with gently flowing 5μm filtered seawater. Before the dishes are flushed, check to see if any medusae have been released overnight.

••

Sometimes more medusae are produced if the cultures are left undisturbed for three to four days at a time.

••

• *Species compatibility*: They may be displayed together with sea gooseberries (*Pleurobrachia* sp.) and cross jellies (*Mitrocoma cellularia*).

Table 7.6. Suggested diet for
bell jellies (*Eutonina indicans*)

Life history stage	Food type	Feeding frequency	Recommended amount
Large medusae (Phase III) > 15mm	Artemia nauplii Wild plankton	Daily As available	200–350 mL Whatever you have
Small medusae (Phase II) < 15mm	Artemia nauplii Rotifers	Daily Daily	150 mL 100 mL
Newly released medusae (Phase I) New medusa to eight-tentacles stage	Artemia nauplii Rotifers	Daily Daily	25 mL 25 mL
Polyps	Rotifers	Daily	25 mL

Further reading:

Abbot, D. P. Observing Marine Invertebrates: Drawings from the laboratory (Stanford, CA: Stanford
University Press, 1987).

Boero, F. 1987. Life cycles of *Phialella zappai* n. sp.,
Phialella fragilis and *Phialella* sp. (Cnidaria, Lep-
tomedusae, Phialellidae) from central California.
Journal of Natural History 21(2):465–480.

Larson, R. J. 1987. Respiration and carbon turnover
rates of medusae from the NE Pacific. *Comparative biochemistry and physiology* 87(1):93–100.

Rutherford, R. D., and E. V. Thuesen. 2005. Metabolic performance and survival of medusae in
estuarine hypoxia. *Marine Ecology Progress Series*
294:189–200.

Werner, B. 1968. Polypengeneration und entwicklung
von *Eutonina indicans* (Thecata-Leptomedusae).
Helgoland Marine Research 18(4):384–403.

Egg Yolk Jellyfish
(*Phacellophora camtschatica*)

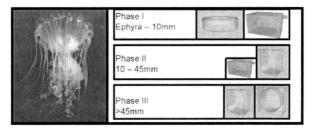

Figure 7.7. *Left,* Egg yolk jelly *(Phacellophora camtschatica)*. *Right,* tanks for growing medusae of *P. camtschatica.* Phase I, eight-inch diameter culture dish without stirrer or screened-in flow-through tank. Phase II, screened-in flow-through tank, one- or two-foot diameter pseudokreisel. Phase III, two-foot diameter pseudokreisel, four- or five-foot round kreisel.

- *Description*: Egg yolk jellies are normally yellow to orange in color and have long, delicate tentacles arranged in bundled clusters around the bell margin. There are also four long frilly and highly folded mouth arms dangling down from the center of the bell.
- *Distribution/range*: Pacific Ocean Kamchatka to Chile, scattered distribution globally.
- *General remarks*: Egg yolk jellies eat all other species of jellies they are physically able to manipulate. And they are capable of removing large amounts of gelatinous prey from volumes of water. About 80% of wild egg yolk jellies from Monterey Bay are infested with parasitic amphipods (*Hyperia medusarum*), and about 65% of them harbor juvenile crabs that hitchhike on jellies. While hitchhiking, the crabs chase and eat parasites.

Wild-collected medusae may for a short time take on the dominant color of the food they have been eating. For example, one year I collected several egg yolk jellies from the field that had been eating black sea nettles (*Chyrsaora achlyos*). Those egg yolk jellies had a dark blackish, purple color about them. Similarly, egg yolk jellies that have been eating Pacific sea nettles (*Chrysaora fuscescens*) are darker orange in color. In the laboratory, when fed *Artemia* nauplii alone, the jellies are pale yellow in color.

Polyps held at 14°C will strobilate on their own in episodic waves every four to five months. To induce strobilation, drop the temperature from 14°C to 10°C and maintain it there for about three weeks. At the end of three weeks, bring the temperature back up to 14°C. Polyps should strobilate a few weeks later. These polyps don't stay attached to dishes in bright light but are better at it in dim light. Use a plastic-covered pole when cleaning to avoid incidental tentacles sticking to the pole.

•••
Use a plastic-covered pole when cleaning to avoid incidental tentacles sticking to the pole.
•••

About a half hour to forty-five minutes before cleaning the inside of the tank, it's a good practice to feed the egg yolk jellies some moon jellyfish. This causes the jellies to retract their arms and tentacles as they feed. This way you can

avoid tangling and losing tentacles that accidentally stick to the cleaning pole.

Water quality/environment:

Temperature: 8°C–17°C
Salinity: 33 ppt

- *Rearing instructions*: Phase I includes newly released medusae up with a bell diameter up to 10
mm. They will do well in dishes with standing
seawater and given daily water changes. They also
do OK in screened-in flow-through tanks.
    Phase II medusae, measuring from 10–45
mm in diameter, do well in screened-in flow-
through tanks and pseudokreisels.
    Phase III medusae, which are larger than 45
mm in diameter, do well pseudokreisels and kreisels. Move them to a four- or five-foot kreisel
when medusae are about 45 mm in diameter.
- *Species compatibility*: They should be kept as a
single species tank because they will eat other jellyfish.

Table 7.7. Suggested diet for cultured egg yolk jellies.

Life history stage	Food type	Feeding frequency	Recommended amount
Large medusae (Phase III) > 45 mm	Artemia nauplii Small krill Small or chopped moon jellies Wild plankton	Daily 1–2x per week Daily As available	350–500 mL 3–5 pieces per animal 2–3 small moons each Whatever you have
Small medusae (Phase II) 10–45 mm	Artemia nauplii Rotifers Diced moon jellies	Daily Daily Daily	150 mL 100 mL 1 pipette
Ephyrae (Phase I) Ephyra–10 mm	Artemia nauplii Rotifers Diced moon jellies	Daily Daily Daily	25 mL 25 mL 1 pipette
Polyps	Artemia nauplii Rotifers	Daily Daily	25 mL 25 mL

Further reading:

Gershwin, L. A. 1999. Clonal and population variation in jellyfish symmetry. *Journal of the Marine Biological Association of the United Kingdom* 79:993–1000.

Purcell, J. E. 1991. A review of cnidarians and ctenophores feeding on competitors in the plankton. *Hydrobiologia* 217/17:335–342.

Strand, W. S., and W. M. Hamner. 1988. Predatory behavior of *Phacellophora camtschatica* and size-

selective predation upon *Aurelia aurita* (Scyphozoa: Cnidaria) in Saanich Inlet, British Columbia. *Marine Biology* 99(3):409–114.

Towanda T., and E. V. Thuesen. 2006. Ectosymbiotic
behavior of *Cancer gracilis* and its trophic relationships with its host *Phacellophora camtschatica*
and the parasitoid *Hyperia medusarum*. *Marine
Ecology Progress Series* 315:221–236.

Widmer, C. L. 2006. Lifecycle of *Phacellophora
camtschatica* (Cnidaria: Scyphozoa). *Invertebrate
Biology* 125(2):83–90.

~~~~~~~~~~~

Northeast Pacific Sea Nettle (*Chrysaora fuscescens*)

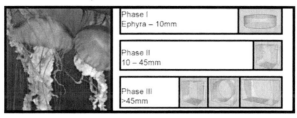

Figure 7.8. *Left*, Pacific sea nettles (*Chrysaora fuscescens*). *Right*, tanks for growing medusae of *Chrysaora fuscescens*. Phase I, eight-inch diameter culture dishes, without a stirrer. Phase II, one-foot diameter pseudokreisels. Phase III, two-foot diameter pseudokreisels, four- or five-foot diameter round kreisel or stretch kreisel.

- *Description*: Cultured young specimens are transparent to orange-brown in bell color. As the medusae get larger, the bell turns darker orange-brown. Some specimens bear stripes reminiscent of the stripes of purple stripe jellies (*Chrysaora colorata*). These medusae typically have a dome shaped bell with long dark brown tentacles surrounding the perimeter. From the center of the bell, four long frilly white mouth arms dangle.
- *Distribution/range*: Mexico to British Columbia.
- *General remarks*: Northeast Pacific sea nettles are large jellyfish that are important players in their ecosystems. They feed on zooplankton and are in turn fed upon by some fish and sea turtles. Hitchhiking symbiotic organisms include juvenile slender crabs (*Cancer gracilis*), medusae fish (*Icichthys lockingtoni*), and butterfish (*Peprilus simillimus*). These

sea nettles are typically found in the Monterey Bay, California, from summer to late fall.

Polyps of *C. fuscescens* are relatively large. They grow slowly, but cultures are long-lived having been maintained for over ten years in the laboratory. These polyps form distinctive cysts at their bases that are attached to the substrate. The cysts are called podocysts (foot-cysts), and their job is to asexually reproduce new polyps. Care should be employed so as not to remove the podocysts when cleaning culture dishes because they are the resting or dormant stages from which new polyps will emerge.

Water quality/environment:

Temperature: 8°C–14°C.
Salinity: 33 ppt

- *Rearing instructions*: Phase I includes newly released medusae up to 10 mm in bell diameter. They do well in dishes with standing seawater and also on shaker tables. Feed them rotifers only for the first ten days (until the bell diameter reaches about 5 mm). After that, feed them finely diced slurry of moon jellies, *Artemia* nauplii, and rotifers. Give their grow-out dishes daily water changes.

  Phase II medusae, measuring from 10–45 mm in diameter, do well in one-foot diameter pseudokreisels. Feed the developing jellies rotifers, enriched *Artemia* nauplii, and finely diced moon jellies.

Phase III medusae are larger than 45 mm in diameter and do well in two-foot-tall pseudokreisels, round kreisels, and stretch kreisels.

- *Species compatibility*: They should be kept in a single-species tank. They may be kept with black sea nettles (*C. achlyos*) and purple stripe jellies (*C. colorata*) in the short term (one to two weeks), but *C. fuscescens* will eventually begin to deteriorate in about week three.

Table 7.8. Suggested laboratory diet for cultured northeast Pacific sea nettles (*Chrysaora fuscescens)*

Life history stage	Food type	Feeding frequency	Recommended amount
Large medusae (Phase III) > 45 mm	Artemia nauplii	Daily	350–500 mL
	Small krill	2–3x per week	10–15 pieces each
	Small or chopped moon jellies	Daily	2–3 small moons each
	Krill shake	1x per week	150 mL per tank
	Wild plankton	As available	Whatever you have
Small medusae (Phase II) 10–45 mm	Artemia nauplii	Daily	250 mL
	Rotifers	Daily	100 mL
	Diced moon jellies	Daily	1 pipette
Ephyrae (Phase I) Ephyra–10 mm	Artemia nauplii	Daily	25 mL
	Rotifers	Daily	25 mL
	Diced moon jellies	Daily	1 pipette
Polyps	Artemia nauplii	Daily	25 mL
	Rotifers	Daily	25 mL

Further reading:

Larson, R. J. 1990. Scyphomedusae and cubomedusae from the eastern Pacific. *Bulletin of Marine
Science* 47(2):546–556.

Shenker, J. M. 1984. Scyphomedusae in surface waters
near the Oregon Coast, May-August, 1981. *Estuarine, Coastal and Shelf Science* 19(6):619–632.

Shenker, J. M. 1985. Carbon content of the neritic
scyphomedusa *Chrysaora fuscescens*. *Journal of
Plankton Research* 7(2):169–173.

Suchman C. L., and R. D. Brodeur. 2005. Abundance
and distribution of large medusae in surface waters of the northern California Current. *Deep-Sea
Research II* 52:51–72.

Widmer, C. L. 2008. Life cycle of *Chrysaora fuscescens*
Brandt, 1835 (Cnidaria: Scyphozoa) with a key
to sympatric ephyrae. *Pacific Science* 62(1):71–82.

Crystal Jelly (*Aequorea victoria*)

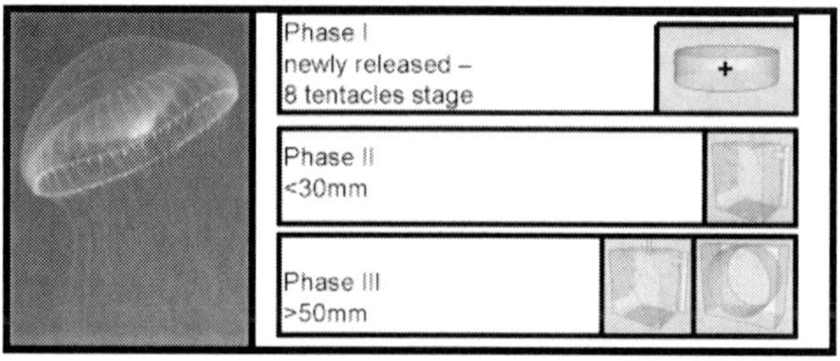

Figure 7.9. *Left*, crystal jelly (*Aequorea victoria*). *Right*, tanks for growing medusae of *Aequorea*. Phase I, eight-inch diameter culture dish with a stirrer. Phase II, one-foot diameter pseudokreisel. Phase III, two-foot diameter pseudokreisel, four- or five-foot round kreisel.

- *Description*: Crystal jellies have a transparent, dome-shaped bell that is wider than it is tall. The gonads are visible as several white lines running down the lengths of the gut canals.
- *Distribution/range*: Bering Sea to southern California. I've seen a different species while I was blue-water diving in the Gulf of California (Sea of Cortez). There are some outstanding unresolved taxonomic questions regarding the genus *Aequorea*, and there are probably several different species of *Aequorea* waiting to be described. Each will have similar husbandry requirements with differing water quality parameters (e.g., temperature and salinity).
- *General remarks*: In Monterey Bay, they are usually present during spring. These jellies are near the top of the food chain as far as surface cruising hydromedusae are concerned. They eat small

moon jellies and will also cannibalize one another. If you overstock a tank with *Aequorea*, they will eat one another until a balanced stocking density is reached.

Aequorea medusae spawn after exposure to light following ten to twelve hours of darkness. Some species of *Aequorea* can asexually reproduce additional medusae by the medusa dividing in half, resulting in two medusae. However, not all members of the genus have been observed to asexually reproduce medusae in this way.

Water quality/environment:

Temperature: 6ºC–15ºC
Salinity: 33 ppt

- *Rearing instructions*: Phase I consists of newly released medusae up to the eight tentacles stage. They do well in dishes with stirred seawater using a plus-shaped magnetic stir bar and given daily water changes. Feed them rotifers for the first two weeks. After that, include a small amount of *Artemia* nauplii mixed in with the rotifers.

   Phase II medusae, meaning those with eight to thirty-two tentacles, do well in one-inch diameter pseudokreisels. Feed them *Artemia* nauplii daily.

   Phase III medusae with more than thirty-two tentacles do well in two-foot diameter pseudokreisels and four- and five-foot diameter round kreisels.
- *The Hydroid:* Hydroids should be maintained in

dishes with standing seawater resting in temperature-controlled baths at 14°C. Feed them
a small amount of rotifers every other day, and
give them gentle water changes each day. Water
changes should be done by flushing the cultures
with gently flowing seawater. Before the dishes
are flushed, check to see if any medusae are present. More medusae seem to be produced if the
cultures are left undisturbed for three to four days
at a time.

Table 7.9. Suggested diet for cultured crystal jellies
(*Aequorea* sp.)

Life history stage	Food type	Feeding frequency	Recommended amount
Large medusae (Phase III) > 50 mm	Artemia nauplii Wild plankton	Daily As available	200–350 mL Whatever you have
Small medusae (Phase II) < 30 mm	Artemia nauplii Rotifers	Daily Daily	150 mL 100 mL
Newly released medusae (Phase I) New medusa to eight-tentacles stage	Rotifers	Daily	25 mL
Polyps	Rotifers	Daily	25 mL

Further reading:

Arai, M. N. 1986. Oxygen consumption of fed and
starved *Aequorea victoria* (Murbach and Shearer,

1902) (Hydromedusae). *Physiological Zoology* 59(2):188–193. Arai, M. N. 1991. Attraction of *Aurelia* and *Aequorea* to prey. *Hydrobiologia* 216/17(1):363–366.

Buecher, E., C. Sparks, A. Brierley, H. Boyer, and M. Gibbons. 2001. Biometry and size distribution of *Chrysaora hysoscella* (Cnidaria, Scyphozoa) and *Aequorea aequorea* (Cnidaria, Hydrozoa) off Namibia with some notes on their parasite *Hyperia medusarum*. *Journal of Plankton Research* 23(10):1073–1080.

Kendall, J. L., and M. N. Badminton. 1998. *Aequorea victoria* bioluminescence moves into an exciting new era. *Trends in biotechnology* 16(5):216–224.

Purcell, J. E. 1991. Predation by *Aequorea victoria* on other species of potentially competing pelagic hydrozoans. *Marine Ecology Progress Series* 72:255–260.

Black Sea Nettle (*Chrysaora achlyos*)

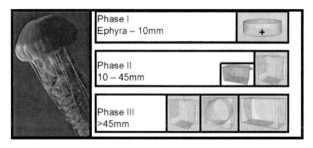

Figure 7.10. *Left*, the black sea nettle (*Chrysaora achlyos*). *Right*, tanks for growing medusae of the black sea nettle (*C. achlyos*). Phase I, eight-inch diameter culture dish with a stirrer. Phase II, screened-in flow-through tank, one-foot diameter pseudokreisel. Phase III, two-foot diameter pseudokreisel, four- or five-foot round kreisel, stretch kreisel.

- *Description*: A large, deep purple to blackish medusa of *Chrysaora* body form. Small, cultured specimens are more maroon in color and become a dark blackish-purple with age. Cultured ones sometimes develop stripes and sometimes they do not.
- *Distribution/range*: Unknown, but they at least probably live off Baja California, Mexico. Warm El Niño currents have carried the medusae as far north as Monterey, California.
- *General remarks*: This large, enigmatic jelly was only recently scientifically described. The main reason such a large medusa escaped attention was that it only appears sporadically, often in association with El Niño events. When they arrive in masses, they cause a commotion because they can get really big, up to 1.5 meters across. Small fish

associate with them, as well as the usual parasitic amphipods and mutualistic crabs.

Of the cultured *Chrysaora* species, these appear to be one of the easiest and fastest to grow. However, once damaged they go down hill quickly and generally do not recover.

Water quality/environment:

Temperature: 15ºC–25ºC

Salinity: 33 ppt

- *Rearing instructions*: Phase I consists of newly released ephyrae, up to 10 mm in bell diameter. The medusae do well in dishes with stirred seawater and also on shaker tables. Feed them rotifers and microdiced moon jellies until they reach bell diameters of about 5 mm. Perform daily water changes.

    Phase II medusae measure from 10–45 mm in diameter and do well in screened-in flow-through tanks and one- and two-foot tall pseudokreisels. Feed them the same foods as phase I medusae and include larger moon jelly chunks.

    Phase III medusae are larger than 45 mm in diameter and do well in two-foot diameter pseudokreisels, four- and five-foot tall round kreisels and stretch kreisels.

- *Species compatibility*: They may be kept with the purple striped jelly (*Chrysaora colorata*).

Table 7.10. Suggested diet for cultured black sea nettles (*Chrysaora achlyos*)

Life history stage	Food type	Feeding frequency	Recommended amount
Large medusae (Phase III) > 45 mm	Artemia nauplii	Daily	500–1000 mL
	Small krill	2–3x per week	10–15 pieces each
	Small or chopped moon jellies	Daily	2–3 small moons each
	Krill shake	1x per week	200 mL per tank
	Wild plankton	As available	Whatever you have
Small medusae (Phase II) 10–45 mm	Artemia nauplii	Daily	250 mL
	Rotifers	Daily	100 mL
	Diced moon jellies	Daily	2 pipettes
Ephyrae (Phase I) Ephyra–10 mm	Artemia nauplii	Daily	25 mL
	Rotifers	Daily	25 mL
	Diced moon jellies	Daily	1 pipette
Polyps	Artemia nauplii	Daily	25 mL
	Rotifers	Daily	25 mL

Further reading:

Martin, J. W., and H. G. Kuck. 1991. Faunal associates of an undescribed species of *Chrysaora* (Cnidaria, Scyphozoa) in the Southern California Bight, with notes on unusual occurrences of other warm water species in the area. *Bulletin of Southern California Academy of Sciences* 90(3):89–101.

Martin, J. W., L. A. Gershwin, J. W. Burnett, D. G. Cargo, and D. A. Bloom. 1997. *Chrysaora achlyos*, a Remarkable New Species of Scyphozoan from the Eastern Pacific. *The Biological Bulletin* 193(1)8–13.

Morandini A. C., F. da Silveira, and G. Jarms. 2004. The life cycle of *Chrysaora lactea* Eschscholtz, 1829 (Cnidaria, Scyphozoa) with notes on the scyphistoma stage of three other species. *Hydrobiologia* 530/531:347–354.

Radwana, F. Y., L. A. Gershwin, and J. W. Burnnett. 2000. Toxinological studies on the nematocyst venom of *Chrysaora achlyos*. *Toxicon* 38(11)1581–1591.

Schaadt, M., L. Yasukochi, L. A. Gershwin, and D. Wrobel. 2000. Husbandry of the black jelly (*Chrysaora achlyos*), a newly discovered scyphozoan in the eastern North Pacific Ocean. *Bulletin de l'Institut océanographique* 20(1):289–296.

Black Star Northern Sea Nettle (*Chrysaora melanaster*)

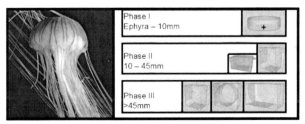

Figure 7.11. *Left*, the black star northern sea nettle (*Chrysaora melanaster*). *Right*, tanks for growing medusae of the black star sea nettle (*C. melanaster*). Phase I, eight-inch diameter culture dish with a stirrer. Phase II, screened-in flow-through tank or a one-foot diameter pseudokreisel. Phase III, two-foot diameter pseudokreisel, four- or five-foot diameter round kreisel, stretch kreisel.

- *Description*: A large medusa of *Chrysaora* body form with a dark radiating star pattern on the exumbrella.
- *Distribution/range*: Bering Sea
- *General remarks*: Be careful not to damage the tentacles and oral arms of this species. They can get quite long, tangle easily, and are very delicate. When the tentacles and oral arms are torn away they don't regenerate quickly.

Water quality/environment:

Temperature: 10ºC–14ºC
Salinity: 33 ppt

- *Rearing instructions*: Phase I consists of newly released medusae up to 10 mm in bell diameter. They do well in dishes with stirred seawater and also on shaker tables. Feed them rotifers and microdiced moon jellies until the bell diameter reaches about 5 mm. After that, include *Artemia* nauplii in their diet. Give them daily water changes.

Phase II medusae measure from 10–45 mm in diameter and do well in screened-in flow-through tanks and one-foot diameter pseudokreisels. Feed them the same food as above and include larger moon jelly chunks. Move them to a four- or five-foot diameter kreisel when the medusae reach 45 mm in diameter.

Phase III medusae are larger than 45 mm in diameter and do well in two-foot diameter pseudokreisels, four- and five-foot diameter round kreisels, and stretch kreisels.

- *Species compatibility*: They should be kept as a single species.

96   how to keep jellyfish in aquariums

Table 7.11. Suggested diet for cultured black star sea nettles *(Chrysaora melanaster)*.

Life history stage	Food type	Feeding frequency	Recommended amount
Large medusae (Phase III) > 45 mm	Artemia nauplii	Daily	500–1000 mL
	Small krill	2–3x per week	10–15 pieces each
	Small or chopped moon jellies	Daily	2–3 small moons each
	Krill shake	1x per week	150 mL per tank
	Wild plankton	As available	Whatever you have
Small medusae (Phase II) 10–45 mm	Artemia nauplii	Daily	200 mL
	Rotifers	Daily	100 mL
	Diced moon jellies	Daily	4 pipettes
Ephyrae (Phase I) Ephyra–10 mm	Artemia nauplii	Daily	25 mL
	Rotifers	Daily	25 mL
	Diced moon jellies	Daily	1 pipette
Polyps	Artemia nauplii	Daily	25 mL
	Rotifers	Daily	25 mL

Further reading:

Brodeur, R. D. 1998. In situ observations of the association between juvenile fishes and scyphomedusae in the Bering Sea. *Marine Ecology Progress Series* 163:11–20.

Brodeur, R. D., H. Sugisaki, and G. L. Hunt. 2002. Increases in jellyfish biomass in the Bering Sea: implications for the ecosystem. *Marine Ecology Progress Series* 233:89–103.

Fukushi, K., N. Ishio, J. Tsujimoto, K. Yokota, T. Hamatake, H. Sogabe, K. Toriya, and T. Ninomiya. 2004. Preliminary study on the potential usefulness of jellyfish as fertilizer. *Bulletin of the Society of Sea Water Science, Japan* 58(2):209–217.

Kinoshital, J., J. Hiromi, and Y. Yamada. 2006. Abundance and biomass of scyphomedusae, *Aurelia aurita* and *Chrysaora melanaster*, and Ctenophora, *Bolinopsis mikado*, with estimates of their feeding impact on zooplankton in Tokyo Bay, Japan. *Journal of Oceanography* 62(5):607–615.

Purcell, J. E., and M. B. Decker. 2005. Effects of climate on relative predation by scyphomedusae and ctenophores on copepods in Chesapeake Bay during 1987–2000. *Limnology and Oceanography* 50(1):376–387.

Purple Striped Jellyfish
(*Chrysaora colorata*)

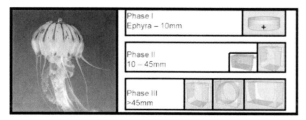

Figure 7.12. *Left*, purple striped jellyfish (*Chrysaora colorata*). The specimen pictured here has two symbiotic barnacles on top of the bell. *Right*, tanks for growing medusae of *Chrysaora colorata*. Phase I, eight-inch diameter culture dish with a stirrer. Phase II, screened-in flow-through tank, one-foot diameter pseudokreisel. Phase III, two-foot diameter pseudokreisel, four- or five-foot diameter round kreisel, stretch kreisel.

- *Description*: Young, cultured specimens are pinkish in color. They don't develop their purple stripes until they reach about 12 cm in diameter. Wild specimens show the same pattern regarding stripe development and size.
- *Distribution/range*: Bodega Bay through San Pedro Basin, southern California.
- *General remarks*: *C. colorata* are large, conspicuous jellyfish that feed on zooplankton and are in turn fed upon by some fish and sea turtles. Several symbiotic organisms use *C. colorata* as hosts including juvenile crabs, medusae fish, butterfish, barnacles, and hydroids of other jellyfish species (*Obelia* sp.).

Tapping medusae on the bell evokes a run response whereby they turn downward and increase bell pulsing frequencies (to perhaps four times the relaxed rate).

Keep the polyps at 18°C–22°C for general, long-term maintenance. To induce strobilation, lower the temperature to 15°C. Strobilae should form in about three to five weeks. When you have met your ephyra production needs, return the tank temperature to 21°C. If you continue to maintain this species at strobilation temperatures, the polyps will eventually stop producing viable ephyrae.

Water quality/environment:
Temperature: 15°C–21ºC
Salinity: 33 ppt

• *Rearing instructions*: Phase I consists of newly released medusae up to 10 mm in bell diameter. They do well in dishes with stirred seawater and also on shaker tables. Feed them rotifers for the first ten days (until the bell diameter reaches about 5 mm) and minced moon jellies. Give them daily water changes. After ten days, the jellies should be large enough to add *Artemia* nauplii to their diet.

Phase II medusae measure from 10–45 mm in diameter and do well in screened-in flow-through tanks and one-foot diameter pseudokreisels. Feed them *Artemia* nauplii daily and add small chopped moon jellies to their diet.

Phase III medusae are larger than 45 mm in diameter and do well in two-foot diameter pseudokreisels, four- and five-foot diameter round kreisels, and stretch kreisels.

• *Species compatibility*: May be kept with the black sea nettle (*Chrysaora achlyos*).

Table 7.12. Suggested diet for cultured purple striped jellies *(Chrysaora colorata).*

Life history stage	Food type	Feeding frequency	Recommended amount
Large medusae (Phase III) > 45 mm	Artemia nauplii	Daily	500–1000 mL
	Small krill	2–3x per week	10–15 pieces each
	Small or chopped moon jellies	Daily	2–3 small moons each
		1x per week	
	Krill shake	As available	150 mL per tank
	Wild plankton		Whatever you have
Small medusae (Phase II) 10–45 mm	Artemia nauplii	Daily	250 mL
	Rotifers	Daily	100 mL
	Diced moon jellies	Daily	4 pipettes
Ephyrae (Phase I) Ephyra–10 mm	Artemia nauplii	Daily	25 mL
	Rotifers	Daily	25 mL
	Diced moon jellies	Daily	1 pipette
Polyps	Artemia nauplii	Daily	25 mL
	Rotifers	Daily	25 mL

Further reading:

Gershwin, L. A., and A. G. Collins. 2002. A preliminary phylogeny of Pelagiidae (Cnidaria, Scyphozoa), with new observations of *Chrysaora colorata* comb. nov. *Journal of Natural History* 36:127–148.

Widmer, C. L. 2005. Jellyfish population trends in Southern Monterey Bay, California from 2000–2005. *Ecosystem Observations for the Monterey Bay National Marine Sanctuary*:11–12.

Widmer, C. L., J. P. Voorhees, M. A. Badger, J. W. Lambert, and N. M. Block, 2005. The effects of rearing vessels and laboratory diets on growth of Northeast Pacific jellyfish ephyrae (Cnidaria: Scyphozoa). *Drum and Croaker* 36:29–36.

Wrobel, D., and C. E. Mills. 1998. Pacific coast pelagic invertebrates: a guide to the common gelatinous animals. *Sea Challengers/Monterey Bay Aquarium, Monterey*

Cross Jelly (*Mitrocoma cellularia*)

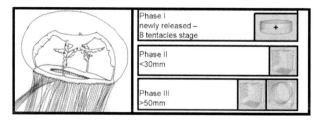

Figure 7.13. *Left*, cross jelly (*Mitrocoma cellularia*). *Right*, tanks for growing medusae of *Mitrocoma cellularia*. Phase I, eight-inch diameter culture dish with a stirrer. Phase II, one-foot diameter pseudokreisel. Phase III, two-foot diameter pseudokreisel, four- or five-foot diameter round kreisel.

Description: Specimens have a transparent bell that is wider than it is tall with gonads that are visible as four long straight white tubes running down the lengths of the gut canals.

- *Distribution/range*: Bering Sea to southern California.
- *General remarks*: Cross jellies live in deep water, but are sometimes found on the surface. Their transparency probably helps them avoid predators by acting as a kind of camouflage. They are eaten by other kinds of jellyfish and are parasitized by larvae of *Peachia*—a sea anemone—and also amphipods. They are bioluminescent (can make their own blue-green colored light), although the function of their bioluminescence is unknown. Specimens grown under laboratory conditions do not bioluminesce because laboratory raised live foods lack the chemicals needed by the jellyfish for building light-making molecules.

Medusae may be deleteriously affected by bright light, and they are prone to going downhill after being banged around by cleaning tools during maintenance.

Mitrocoma cellularia medusae spawn after exposure to light following ten to twelve hours of darkness.

Colonies maintained at 10°C produce medusae in regular and predictable waves about every forty-five days.

Water quality/environment:

Temperature: 5°C–15ºC
Salinity: 33 ppt
Light levels: They prefer low light levels.

• *Rearing instructions*: Phase I includes newly released medusae up to the eight-tentacles stage of development. The medusae do well in dishes with stirred seawater using a plus-shaped stirrer. Feed them rotifers only until medusae reach the eight-tentacles stage and remember to give them daily water changes. After they reach the eight-tentacles stage, add a small amount of *Artemia* nauplii to the diet.

Phase II medusae, or those having eight to thirty-two tentacles, do well in one-foot diameter pseudokreisels. Feed them *Artemia* nauplii and rotifers daily.

Phase III medusae have more than thirty-two tentacles do well in two-foot diameter pseudokreisels and four- and five-foot diameter round kreisels. Feed them *Artemia* nauplii daily and adult *Artemia* three times per week.

Feed the hydroid colony rotifers only. *Artemia* nauplii are too large for hydranths in the colony to manage.

- *Species compatibility*: May be kept with bell jellies (*Eutonina indicans*).

Table 7.13. Suggested diet for cultured cross jellies
(Mitrocoma cellularia).

Life history stage	Food type	Feeding frequency	Recommended amount
Large medusae (Phase III) > 50 mm	Artemia nauplii Wild plankton	Daily As available	200–350 mL Whatever you have
Small medusae (Phase II) < 30 mm	Artemia nauplii Rotifers	Daily Daily	150 mL 100 mL
Newly released medusae (Phase I) New medusa to 8-tentacles stage	Rotifers	Daily	25 mL
Polyps	Rotifers	Daily	25 mL

Further reading:

Colin, S., J. H. Costello, and E. Klos. 2003. In situ swimming and feeding behavior of eight co-occurring hydromedusae. *Marine Ecology Progress Series* 253:305–309.

Costello, J. H., and S. P. Colin. 2002. Prey resource use by coexistent hydromedusae from Friday Harbor, Washington. *Limnology and oceanography* 47(4):934–942.

Mills, C. E. 1993. Natural mortality in NE Pacific coastal hydromedusae: Grazing predation, wound healing and senescence. *Bulletin of Marine Science* 53(1):194–203.

Tamburri, M. N., M. N. Magdalena, and B. H. Robison. 2000. Chemically Regulated Feeding by a Midwater Medusa. *Limnology and Oceanography* 45(7):1661–1666.

Widmer, C. L. 2004. The hydroid and early medusa stages of *Mitrocoma cellularia* (Hydrozoa, Mitrocomidae). *Marine Biology* 145:315–321.

Lobed Comb Jellies

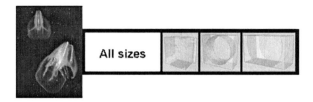

Figure 7.14. *Left*, comb jellies (*Mnemiopsis*). *Right*, tanks
for maintaining all kinds of comb jellies, two-foot diameter
pseudokreisels, four- or five-foot diameter round kreisels, and
stretch kreisels.

- *Description*: Comb jellies have eight ciliated comb
  rows that diffract white light, resulting in a rainbow effect, making them charismatic display animals. They have four oral lobes that can open, two
  up and two down, when fishing for zooplankton.
  The lobes are retracted when the animal wishes
  to swim away quickly. Some possess two thin
  trailing tentacles that may be retracted or extended. The function of the two small tentacles
  is unknown. When present, four auricles (they
  look sort of like tentacles) move in asynchronous
  waves, reminding me of a breakdancer from the
  1980s doing the "wave."
- *General remarks*: Lobate ctenophores swim slowly,
  trapping zooplankton on their large oral lobes.
  Food is slowly passed along ciliated grooves to
  the mouth. *Leucothea* and *Bolinopsis* are native
  to the Monterey Bay, but *Mnemiopsis* are not.
  Where *Mnemiopsis* have been successfully introduced as a non-native species, they have eaten

fish eggs with crippling effects on the food chain. It is imperative that *Mnemiopsis* and the water used to maintain them are not released into the ocean.

Very little is known about the ecology or biology of the orange-spotted comb jelly (*Leucothea pulchra*) due to the extreme fragility of these animals.

••
The animals are very delicate, sometimes currents from a passing diver's hand are sufficient to render them to pieces.
••

Smaller lobed comb jellies (softball sized) do better in captivity than larger ones (ones the size of a loaf of bread). Use all the caution you can muster when handling them or they will disintegrate. They are able to regenerate lost parts as long as the holding tank and feeding requirements are optimal.

Water quality/environment:

Temperature for maintaining: *Leucothea* or *Mnemiopsis* 15˚C–21˚C
Temperature for maintaining: *Bolinopsis* 5˚C–17˚C
Salinity: 33ppt

• *Rearing instructions*: Large-scale batch culture methods are unreliable at present. To maintain them, it is imperative that the tank currents are adjusted properly. Be sure to bleach your holding tanks before adding lobed comb jellies because if there are any fouling hydroids present, they will

cause significant damage to the collection in a
very short time.
• *Species compatibility*: Keep them in a single-species tank.

Table 7.14. Suggested diet for captive
lobed comb jellies.

Life history stage	Food type	Feeding frequency	Recommended amount
All stages	Artemia nauplii	Daily	350–500 mL
	Live small krill	As available	3–5 each
	Fish eggs	As available	

Further reading:

Baker, L. D., and M. R. Reevel. 1974. Laboratory
culture of the lobate ctenophore

Mnemiopsis mccradyi with notes on feeding and fecundity. *Marine Biology* 26(1): 57–62.

Costello, J. H., and R. Coverdale. 1998. Planktonic
feeding and evolutionary significance of the lobate body plan within the Ctenophora. *Biological
Bulletin* 195(2):247–248.

Matsumoto, G. I. 1988. A new species of lobate
ctenophore, *Leucothea pulchra* sp. nov., from the
California Bight. *Journal of Plankton Research*
10(2):301–311.

Nagabhushanam, A. K., 1950. Feeding of a ctenophore, *Bolinopsis Infundibulum* (O. F. Müller). *Nature* 184:829.

Thuesen, E. V., D. Ladd, Rutherford, and P. L. Brommer. 2005. The role of aerobic metabolism and intragel oxygen in hypoxia tolerance of three ctenophores: *Pleurobrachia bachei, Bolinopsis infundibulum* and *Mnemiopsis leidyi. Journal of the Marine Biological Association of the UK* 85:627–633.

New-to-You Jellyfish and the Clues They Provide

What if you go out into the world and find a jellyfish species that is new to you, or new to science? How should you proceed if you wish to keep the specimens alive in order to learn from them? When dealing with small specimens with unknown husbandry requirements, I use the care requirements given for the cross jelly (*Mitrocoma cellularia*). If the animals are larger and look delicate, I use the methods described above for lobed comb jellies. When dealing with wild-caught specimens, the following questions should direct you down the correct jelly husbandry path:

- Where did you find your new jelly?
- What was the water temperature?
- What was the salinity?
- How about the amount of dissolved oxygen in the water?
- Was the jelly eating anything when you found it?
- Could you observe anything in the gut that may give dietary clues?
- Can you start a culture of them so you can work with more in the future?

Things to Think About Before Acquiring Jellies

1. Make sure the tank is ready to receive them, and the water is properly mixed and at the correct temperature. The system is able to function in its "normal" mode and has done so for at least a week without any leaks or other minor catastrophes.

2. How will you treat your seawater when you are finished using it? Is it OK to send the seawater into the sewer in your town?

3. Do you really want a certain jellyfish over another one? Consider the ease of care in terms of feeding and longevity, etc. Are they affordable?

4. Were the jellies collected from the wild, or were they cultured? You may be able to eventually culture your own jellies, thus decreasing your overall costs.

5. Is the vendor/collector reputable? If you are buying online, does the vendor have a "what you see is what you get" section on their website? Ask around. Are jellies coming from a particular supplier somehow less desirable than jellies coming from another one?

6. Are the jellies healthy? If you can see them before you purchase them, you can assess their health.

7. Are you prepared to deal with potential fouling organisms (parasites of jellies, etc)?

Part 3
Collections
Management

7

GENERAL RULES OF THUMB

THE FOLLOWING ARE suggested guidelines for general collections management.

1. *Keep the holding tanks clean.* Debris allowed to accumulate in the tank can cause major problems because it acts as a substrate for undesired organisms like hydroids, bacteria, and diatoms. Unwelcome fouling hydroids have stinging tentacles that can damage the skin of jellyfish as they pass by.

2. *Keep the jellies well fed.* Jellyfish need energy to grow and regenerate damaged parts. Wild jellyfish are surrounded by zooplankton all the time so they are constantly feeding on a wide variety of nutritious foods. Captive jellies generally don't eat as often as wild ones, and their diet is not as varied. Therefore, the health of captive jellies can decline over time without proper nutrition. It is

important to feed your jellies regularly with the
best food possible.

3. *You can love them to death.* Put your hands in jelly
   display and culture tanks as infrequently as possible. Only do what is required as excessive handling will cause both jellyfish and their polyp
   cultures to go downhill fast. You can love your
   jellies to death. When it is necessary to work inside tanks, go slowly and try not to bang the jellies. Some species are more tolerant than others,
   but try to keep the unnecessary meddling to a
   minimum.

4. *Increasing temperature increases growth…to a
   point.* All jellyfish species have an operating range
   within which optimal growth is achieved. Within
   physiological tolerances, increasing temperature
   increases growth. If you have a relatively small
   tank, you may want to keep the temperature on
   the lower end of the operating range rather than
   the higher so your jellies don't outgrow the tank
   too quickly. If you have a large tank and want to
   obtain big jellies quickly, feed them a lot and increase the temperature.

5. *What happens if you make a temperature error?*
   When jellies are subjected to temperatures that
   are too high for too long they may become heat
   stressed. Excess heat causes enzymes in the body
   to change shape so they are no longer able to do
   their jobs. This condition ultimately leads to the

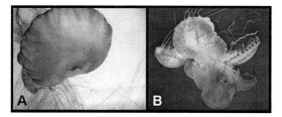

Figure 9.1. Illustration (A) shows a Pacific sea nettle in the middle stages of "hole in the head disease." This jelly is going downhill. Illustration (B) shows tangled purple striped jellies *(Chrysaora colorata)*, caused by overstocking the tank.

demise of the jelly. Heat-shocked jellies generally evert their bells and don't recover. However, if you err on the side of cold shocking the jellies, their growth either slows or the jellies shrink. When the temperature is warmed to the proper degree, the jellies begin to grow again.

6. *Moderate stocking density is better than overstocking.* Stocking density is the relative number of animals kept in a tank. A tank with lots of animals is highly stocked, and one with few animals is correspondingly lowly stocked. Jellies living in tanks with lower stocking density tend to grow faster than jellies grown in tanks that are highly stocked.

7. *Multiple feeds per day are better than one massive feeding.* Jellyfish can only eat so much at one time. Like us, they need time to digest their food and clear their guts before they can eat another meal. Uneaten foods are wasted resources.

8. *Keep components that don't need to be lighted in the dark.* By keeping your system components in the dark you help keep fouling diatoms to a minimum.

8

TROUBLESHOOTING

MORE OFTEN THAN not, it is a suite of issues causing jellies to "get sick." Jellies may be able to get along just fine with two or three stressful factors, but adding one more stressor can overload the healing capacity of the jelly and result in "disease." Finding and correcting the problem sooner than later will greatly enhance your jellies' ability to recover. Well–cared for jellies recover faster and get sick less frequently than poorly cared-for jellies, which may not recover at all.

There is something we jelly-keepers call the health curve. It is shaped like a bell curve. On the left side of the bell curve and at the apex are jellyfish in good condition. Everything on the right side of the bell curve represents sick jellyfish. If the problem-causing disease is identified and rectified while the jelly health is at the apex or maybe one quarter down the right side of the health curve, the jellyfish have a very good chance of recovering. However, if they are allowed to continue more than one third down the health curve, they will do what we in the industry call crap out and "go downhill."

A healthy jellyfish is one that when unfed has relaxed extended tentacles and oral arms. The bell is free from holes, and the margin of the bell is not torn or ratty looking. Healthy jellies in cold water gently pulse every few seconds; in warm water they usually pulse more frequently.

Table 9.1. Signs, symptoms, and possible solutions for commonly encountered challenges in jellyfish aquariums.

Symptom	Possible cause(s)	Possible solutions
The jellies have a clear hole in the center of the bell, or "hole in the head disease"	Poor diet, poor water quality, poorly adjusted current such that the jellies spin on the bottom of the tank for too long before they return in the up current.	Improve the diet, readjust or rebalance the current in the tank, sterilize the tank with bleach.
The jellies have a ratty or torn bell margin	Poor diet, wild medusae may have been preyed upon by medusa fish, captive jellies may be suffering from hydroid and polyp stings or other abrasives in the tanks.	Clean the holding tank of all fouling debris. One may wish to bleach or sterilize the tank. Improve the diet.
The bell is everted; it looks like an umbrella in a windstorm, the tentacles are retracted and don't catch food.	Possibly due to temperature shocking, or could be poor diet, salinity shocking.	Check and adjust the temperature and salinity. There may be hidden fouling organisms in the tank. Bleach the tank.
The epidermis (skin) of the jellies is worn away at the sides only	Are there hydroids, abrasives, or polyps on the tank walls? Are the jellies not being fed frequently enough to regenerate lost parts?	Clean the tank well by bleaching the tank and improve the diet.

Symptom	Possible cause(s)	Possible solutions
The tentacles and oral arms are retracted for extended periods	Did you recently bleach the system and not neutralize it thoroughly? If so, the jellies could be bleach damaged, typically most jellies don't recover from this condition. Have they just been fed? If so this is normal feeding behavior and it will pass when they are finished eating. Check your water quality parameters and adjust them if needed. Have the jellies been getting banged around by cleaning tools at maintenance time?	If the jellies have just been fed they will re-extend their tentacles when they are finished digesting their meal. Otherwise, identify the problem and solve it.
The tentacles and oral arms are gone on wild-caught specimens.	They may have been preyed upon by medusa fish, sea turtles, or Mola mola before the collector got to them. If they still have at least some tentacles remaining around the bell margin, they will probably be able to catch and eat enough food to regenerate lost parts.	They can recover from this condition if well cared for and at least a few of the feeding tentacles remain. Improve the diet.
The bell is flattening out over time (like a dinner plate), and there is very little pulsing.	Poor flow leading to no exercise for the jellyfish. This condition may lead to a flat or plate-shaped bell. If left untreated they will eventually evert. Another possibility is that they may have been stuck to the outflow screen.	Rebalance the tank currents. Improve the diet and check water quality.

Symptom	Possible cause(s)	Possible solutions
Brown coloration covering parts or entire bell.	The jellies are getting old. Or there are too many diatoms in the tank and they are accumulating on the mucus covered bells of the jellies.	Bleach the tank and improve the diet.
The bell of the jellies are doming out, looking more like a ball than a lens.	Too much flow; see the section on proper flow balancing. Have the jellies been getting banged around at maintenance time?	Readjust the tank currents. Jellies that dome out are typically in tanks where the current is too fast and the jellies ride around the perimeter of the tank instead of gently passing through the center of the tank.
There are lots of little holes in the bells	Could be parasitic amphipods, could be poor water quality, could be worms (nematodes, or I've also seen ribbon worms crawling around inside the jelly of wild-caught specimens). There are also trematodes, or parasitic flatworms that infest the gonads of jellies. Their effect, however, is unknown. Did you feed them wild plankton or plankton cubes with jelly stabbers in them (arrow worms or crab zoea). High oxygen content can cause holes in some jellyfish species, too.	If there are external parasites, remove them with forceps or tweezers. Check the oxygen concentration in the tank—is it too high? Adjust the oxygen concentration if needed.
Jellies are shrinking or not growing	Poor diet, poor water quality, keeping them at temperatures outside their operating range. Did you feed them red-colored copepods?	Clean the tank well by bleaching the tank and improve the diet. Check the temperature—it may be too low. Don't feed them red-colored copepods.

Symptom	Possible cause(s)	Possible solutions
Jellyfish have stopped pulsing altogether	Poorly adjusted flow leading to no exercise leads to a flat or plate shaped bell. If left untreated, they will eventually evert. It may also be possible that the jellyfish is dead.	Rebalance the tank currents and improve the diet. Do the tentacles still catch food? If they don't, the jelly may be dead.
Jellyfish have visible parasites on them	They could be amphipods, exumbrellar barnacles, or a number of other things.	Remove the parasites with forceps or tweezers sooner than later.
Polyps are fading and looking weaker and weaker over time	The light entering the tank may be too bright, or it could be due to any of the other polyp-fouling organisms. Poor diet?	Clean the polyp culture, invert the culture dishes on a perforated table, and feed the polyps twice a day.
Taco Bell, or bell folding in half	First look at the center of the jellyfish bell, particularly in wild-collected specimens. Are there any hitchhiking barnacles attached to the bells of the jellyfish? When the barnacles get too large they can fold the jelly bell, leading to mortality for the jelly.	If barnacles or parasitic amphipods are present, remove them with forceps or tweezers. Feed the jellyfish well and it should soon recover.
Air bubbles trapped in the gut of the jelly	Find what is causing the bubbles to become trapped inside the jellies and make that stop. Check the water currents and observe exactly where in the life-support system the bubbles are contacting the jellies.	You can flip the jellies over and work the bubbles out through the mouth or you can use a scalpel and make small incisions near the bubbles and work them out. The skin will heal itself if the animals are well fed, water quality is good, and the tank currents are properly adjusted.

Symptom	Possible cause(s)	Possible solutions
Jelly tentacles keep getting tangled	There may be too many jellies in the tank. Are the jellies being fed foods that are too large? Are several jellies attempting to eat the same piece of food at the same time?	Decrease the stocking density by one or two animals per day until the tangling problem stops. Resist the urge to help them untangle themselves. Often the well-intentioned aquarist who untangles a jelly knot ends up doing more damage than good by tearing tentacles off the jelly. Another thing to try is to skip a feeding for a day and see if they untangle themselves. Sometimes jellies attempt to gang eat a single piece of largish food. Feeding small pieces of food causes less tangling.
But what if they won't untangle themselves?	The tentacles and arms are probably wrapped so tightly around one another that they are effectively knotted together.	Using an acrylic or glass rod, bring the knot of jellies to the surface, choose a jelly on the perimeter of the tangle, and use the rod to gently and slowly lift an oral arm or two out of the water. Gravity will pull the oral arms down, and in this manner they can untwist and untangle.
Jellies keep getting stuck to windows or the back wall (not the outflow screens)	The tank walls are probably covered with a diatom or bacterial film.	Wipe down the inside tank walls or bleach it.
Anemic, thin-looking jellies, pale and transparent when they shouldn't be	Improper diet	Increase feeding amounts and feed them a variety of foods.
Tentacles retracted, weak or no pulsing	Improper salinity	The salinity may be too low (most commonly) check and adjust.

9

GENERAL CHORES

THERE ARE A number of different chores or jelly-keeping maintenance tasks that should be regularly completed for optimal system health. Some, like harvesting and feeding out live foods, are done every day or nearly every day. Other tasks, like starting a new culture or bleaching a display tank, take place every few weeks or months. To determine what maintenance needs to be done on a particular day, look at your jellies' system—I mean carefully observe and listen to what it tells you. It is a lot like a living with a motorcycle—listen to it, and it tells you what it needs. A careful and experienced eye will be able to pick out both jelly-keeping emergencies and the routine maintenance needing to happen. Below follows a list of common jelly-keeping maintenance tasks.

Common Cleaning and Maintenance Tasks

1. Screen brushing; brush display tank outflow screens to enhance flow

2. *Artemia* nauplii harvesting and feeding out

3. Rotifer harvesting and feeding out

4. Chopping and feeding out moon jellies

5. Siphoning uneaten debris from the bottoms of the display tanks

6. Feeding small krill to the jellies

7. Preparing and feeding out krill shake

8. Doing a system check (performing rounds)

9. Look for and remove fouling hydroid colonies that sting and damage jellies

10. Look for and remove fouling polyps of jellyfish in medusa display tanks

11. Water changes in ephyra grow-out culture dishes

12. Check the system water temperature and salinity

13. Collecting new specimens for display or culture

14. Start new cultures

15. Moving polyps from one dish to another

16. Cleaning cultures

17. System bleaching. From easiest to bleach to most challenging to bleach are: ephyrae catch tanks, polyp culture tanks, pseudo kreisels (both one- and two-foot diameter), round kreisels (four- and five-foot diameters), stretch kreisels, and finally large-scale public aquarium exhibit kreisels.

Bleaching Jellyfish Tanks

I know it sounds crazy but, yes, in order to thoroughly clean and decontaminate your jellies' system, bleaching tanks is a necessary part of keeping jellyfish. Bleach helps get rid of fouling organisms that damage jellyfish as they pass by. The most common fouling organisms are hydroids (*Bougainvillia* sp.) and jellyfish polyps (very often *Aurelia* sp.). If you only wipe the fouling polyps down with a brush, you won't get the entire polyp. They regenerate in three to seven days and go back to being a nuisance. Oftentimes, fouling polyps occur in hard-to-see areas inside the tank, and recirculating bleach water is the only remedy.

Follow these steps to bleach tanks. First, remove all the jellyfish from the tank and put them somewhere they won't get temperature shocked. Next, isolate the reservoir (unless you want to bleach it, too) and then add ordinary laundry bleach to the tank water and let it circulate for at least an hour, but not much more than twenty-four hours. This will kill fouling polyps and dissolve the chitinous sheath surrounding hydroids' soft tissues.

I usually use one gallon of 5.25% strength household bleach per 100 gallons of seawater, allowing it to soak for at least one hour before neutralizing. When bleaching larger tanks, I use one gallon of 12% bleach per 100 gallons and allow it to soak for at least two hours before neutralizing.

> •••••••••••••••••••••••••••••••••••••••
> *DANGER: Do not let the bleach circulate through your filter and reservoir unless you want to sterilize them too!*
> •••••••••••••••••••••••••••••••••••••••

To neutralize the 5.25% concentration bleach water, add sodium thiosulfate (commercial dechlorinator) at the amount of about one cup of sodium thiosulfate to one gallon of bleach used (more sodium thiosulfate will be required if you used the 12% bleach). There are three methods to tell whether or not the bleach water has been thoroughly neutralized. First, bleach water is yellow-green in color. When it is completely neutralized, it is clear—if you see any green in the water, add more sodium thiosulfate. Second, bleach water smells like chlorine. When the water is neutralized, it smells like rotten eggs (sulfur smell from the sulfate). If you smell any chlorine at all, add more sodium thiosulfate. Third, you can purchase chlorine test kits from aquarium supply stores online or at your local pet store. The third method is by far the safest.

As you drain the neutralized tank water to the sewer, rinse the tank walls down with fresh or salt water. When there is only an inch or two of water remaining in the tank use a net to remove any debris (usually dead hydroids). If you don't net them out now, you will end up siphoning them out later when they are resuspended. Refill your tank with clean seawater, wipe down the bubbles from the tank walls and windows, and you're just about finished. Wait for about twenty minutes with the currents properly adjusted for the system to normalize. Check the temperature and salinity of the tank water to be sure the system is normalized. Finally, add two or three jellyfish to the display tank and watch them for half an hour. If they relax and start swimming around in good condition then add the rest of the collection to the tank. However, if they quit pulsing or evert their bells and retract their tentacles and oral arms (signs and symptoms of bleach zorching) do not add the rest of the collection to the tank. Add more sodium thiosulfate and let it run through the entire system for a few hours before draining, rinsing, and refilling with clean seawater.

If the prospect of bleaching your system is scary, you're not alone—it scares the heck out of me every time I do it, too. You have an alternative solution: fresh water. Remove your jellies and keep them somewhere safe for a while. Then drain the salt water from the system. Fill it and run it for three or four days with fresh water only. The fresh water will kill most of the hydroids and polyps but won't dissolve the hydroid outer chitinous coverings. So you will need to be extra diligent and try to rinse and scrub them away. Drain the tank and refill it with seawater. Make sure you check and recheck the salinity in the system every few hours for fluctuations.

Part 4
Culture Work

STARTING AND MAINTAINING CULTURES

Life Cycles

LIFE CYCLES OF jellyfish are different from other animals because jellyfish exist in several different morphological life-history states. In addition to the swimming medusa stage, there is also a bottom-living stage consisting of solitary or colonial polyps. The polyp stages asexually reproduce more polyps, or they can switch gears and produce jellyfish medusae as environmental conditions dictate. Jellyfish medusae swim around and sexually reproduce, spreading the range of the species.

Most jellyfish medusae have separate sexes, that is to say there are males individuals and female individuals (fig. 11.1A). The females produce eggs and can either hold onto them or release them into the water. Males either release sperm in mucus strands or as clouds into the water where they encounter the females. Once the eggs are fertilized, they begin developing exponentially to the 64-cell stage (fig. 11.1B). At that point, the cells undergo the process of gastrulation.

Gastrulation is the embryological process whereby germinal layers are formed. From these germinal layers, all other structures in the jelly will eventually develop. For example, one particular group of cells in a given germinal layer will continue to divide and eventually develop into the mouth while another group of cells is destined to become the gut, etc. An embryo that has recently undergone the process of gastrulation is called a planula larva (fig. 11.1C). It is a ciliated, swimming, oblong-shaped larva that to me looks like a fuzzy Tic Tac candy. Under laboratory conditions, the planulae swim around for seven to ten days, settle to the bottom, and then change into polyps or scyphistomae as specialists call them.

Polyps are referred to by specialists according to their condition or state. Polyps differ from one another in the way they reproduce, how the polyps or colonies are arranged, and by the methods they use to produce medusae. Polyps of medusae belonging to the class Scyphozoa are most often solitary (fig. 11.1D and fig. 11.1E). Many make copies of themselves by budding smaller individuals from their bases. Some polyps are capable of producing benthic over wintering bodies called podocysts. If all of the polyps die for some reason, new ones may emerge from the podocysts when conditions improve (fig. 11.1E). Polyps belonging to the class Scyphozoa produce additional

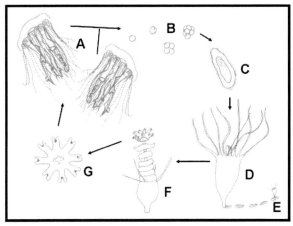

Figure 11.1. Life cycle of a hypothetical scyphozoan jellyfish. Illustration (A) shows mature male and female medusae; (B) shows developing eggs at the two-, four- and eight-cell stages of development (eggs are about one-third of a millimeter wide); (C) shows free-swimming, ciliated planula larva (about 3 mm long); (D) shows a mature polyp (also known as a scyphistoma) about 5 mm tall; (E) shows a podocyst trail in the wake of a polyp; (F) shows a polyp in the strobila stage; and (G) shows a newly released jellyfish, known as an ephyra, measuring about 4 mm across.

medusae by the process of strobilation. When a polyp strobilates, the tentacles of the polyp are absorbed, and the polyp body elongates and forms little discs resembling stacks of flying disc toys (fig. 11.1F). Each disc on the polyp is destined to grow into a jellyfish. The disc eventually begins to flap and breaks free of the bottom-living polyp that generated it. The newly released jelly is called an ephyra (fig. 11.1G).

The number of ephyra produced by a strobilating polyp depends upon the species and how well cared for the polyps were. For example, well–cared for polyps of the northeast Pacific sea nettle (*Chrysaora fuscescens*) have produced up to sixty ephyrae per event, whereas well–cared for egg yolk jelly (*Phacellophora camtschatica*) polyps produced about fifteen ephyrae per strobilation event. If the polyps were poorly cared for, they may only produce one or two ephyrae per event or they may not strobilate at all. After the polyp has finished strobilating, the tentacles are regenerated, a mouth forms, and the polyps begin making asexual copies of themselves once more.

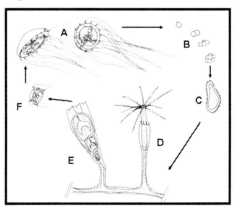

Figure 11.2. Hydrozoan life cycle. Illustration (A) shows adult medusae; (B) shows dividing cells; (C) shows planula larva; (D) shows a feeding polyp (hydranth); (E) shows a medusa-producing polyp (gonangium); and (F) shows newly released medusa.

Jellyfish belonging to the class Hydrozoa have bottom-living polyps that usually form colonies. Among the colonies are different kinds of polyps, each with different jobs. There are feeding polyps called hydranths, and there are medusa-producing polyps called gonangia (fig. 11.2D and fig. 11.2E). Hydranths catch food, which is shared with the entire colony through a series of interconnecting tubes. Medusa-producing polyps are capable of producing one to a few dozen medusae at a time, depending on the species. The variety of form in hydrozoan colonies is staggering and supremely interesting. And there is a lot of room for new scientists in this understudied field.

Obtaining Planulae/Starting Cultures

There are a few methods one can use to start new cultures. One method is to collect several mature medusae from the field and put them all together in the same bag. Allow them to sit overnight, then use a pipette the next day to collect water from the corners of the shipping bags. Jellies in bags often release at least some gametes overnight. When gametes are released into plastic collection bags, fertilization often also takes place. Another method is to order some jellies from a collector, then check the corners of the shipping bags for planulae when they arrive.

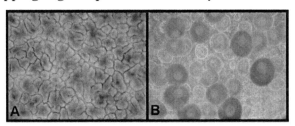

Figure 11.3. Illustration (A) depicts male reproductive parts, the spermatorphores; (B) depicts female reproductive parts, including the ovary with eggs.

A slightly more challenging method is to use *in vitro* fertilization techniques. Again, start by collecting mature male and female jellies. You can collect jellyfish from the wild, purchase them, or grow your own. Dissect out a small portion of mature gonad from both the male and female jellies (fig. 11.3). If you accidentally remove some extra tissue (gut filaments, body wall, etc.) carefully dissect them away and discard them before moving on to the next step. Place the gonads together in a clean glass dish filled with seawater and leave them there until the eggs have been fertilized and planulae have formed. This generally takes about three days.

The planulae generally swim around for three to ten days, then they do a spirally dance of site selection, attach to the bottom, and metamorphose into polyps. Some species have planulae that prefer to settle on the undersides of the water surface rather than the bottom of a glass dish. When that happens, float a smaller glass dish on the surface of the initial glass dish. Planulae will settle on the bottom of the floating glass dish. If the planulae continue to swim for days without ever settling, try increasing the temperature a few degrees, which may help cue them to settle.

How to Maintain Polyps

There are two methods for maintaining polyps that have worked well for me. One method is to keep the polyps in small, covered culture dishes in a temperature-controlled room, for example a refrigerator. They are covered to keep the water from evaporating. The second method—and the one I prefer—is to grow the polyps on dishes and keep the dishes inside an aquarium with water flowing through it. The flow-through method has the benefit of allowing uneaten

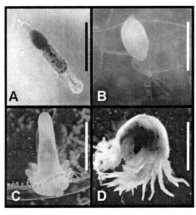

Figure 11.4. Illustration (A) shows small, segmented polychaete worms, which can foul jellyfish polyp cultures. Illustration (B) shows a small flatworm that eats the tentacle crowns of hydroids. Remove them from your cultures whenever you encounter them. Scale bars (A) and (B) = 1 mm. Illustration (C) is a juvenile anemone (*Peachia*) that parasitizes the gonads of hydrozoan jellies. Illustration (D) is a parasitic amphipod; these swim from host to host, eating holes in the jellies' bells. Scale bars (C) and (D) = 2 mm.

food to wash out of the aquarium, and overall water quality remains high with less effort. If you over feed covered culture dishes without giving the dishes good water changes, the dish water can become fouled and the polyps will die.

When maintaining polyps in an aquarium with water flowing through, I like to either set the dishes on their sides or upside down on perforated tables. This arrangement allows the polyps to relax and extend their tentacles and thus feed effectively. It also has the benefit of allowing egested food (polyp poop) to fall to the aquarium floor, making the culture aquarium easier to clean and improving the health of the polyps. If you place dishes open side up, the polyp poop lands around the bases of the polyps, providing all kinds of nasty fouling organisms, including bacterial mats, a place to grow. If debris is allowed to accumulate, the polyps will perish.

How to Move Polyps

If you find yourself wanting to start even more cultures of polyps once your initial dishes are doing well, or you want to share jellyfish polyps with other aquarists, you will need to move polyps. Using a pipette or glass slide, or some other sharp, flat object, gently and evenly scrape along the bottom of the polyp dish until the desired number of polyps accumulate on the scraper edge. Next, pipette the polyps from the scraper edge to a holding dish of clean seawater. Place a clean culture dish in a clean aquarium with seawater gently flowing through it. This one is waiting to receive the freshly scraped polyps. Pipette some of the scraped polyps into the waiting dish. Leave them alone for at least seven days and don't feed them. After seven days, it is OK to gently turn the dish over and allow the polyps to hang and relax their tentacles. Collect any polyps that have fallen to the bottom of the aquarium and attempt to resettle them in a different glass dish. Now it is OK to feed the polyps that have reattached to the new dish. You can also resettle polyps in covered, undisturbed culture dishes in a temperature-controlled room, but I have had best luck using the flow through method.

•••
Only about 40% of the polyps reattach to the new dishes in my experience.
•••

Common Fouling Organisms

Just maintaining jellyfish medusae can be challenging enough, but there is yet another group of
gremlins to consider when maintaining cultures.
Fouling organisms are any living thing that makes
your operation less productive. They usually come in
one of two forms: ones that affect your cultures, and
ones that affect your medusae. The fouling organisms
in cultures tend to be tiny animals that overgrow and
kill or eat your hard-earned polyps. Polyps of *Aurelia*
and *Cassiopeia* tend to be very aggressive, and if they
invade a culture of another species, they will overgrow
and kill the other polyps. So it is important to recog-
nize and remove them as soon as you see them. Don't
put off culture cleaning work or you will be sorry.

The other band of fouling bandits are the ones
riding around on medusae. Some of the hitchhikers
on jellyfish are beneficial, but most of them are not.
Slender crabs (*Cancer gracilis*) hitchhike on jellies as
juveniles and wander around eating parasites they
encounter. Crabs in the wild eventually jump off the
jellyfish. If the crabs in exhibits are allowed to grow
larger than one inch in carapace width, the sharp
ends of the crab legs begin digging in and damaging
the jellies' bells.

Table 11.1. Common fouling organisms affecting cultures and medusae

Fouling organism	What they do	Possible solutions
Diatoms on the culture dishes	They serve as substrate for other fouling organisms to live around. Diatoms can also overgrow your polyps.	Gently remove the diatoms with a small paintbrush. Keep the polyps in the dark or dim light to limit diatom growth.
Ciliates on culture dishes	They swim around and eat at the bases of polyps. They also get into the tubes of hydroids and wreak havoc.	Put the culture dishes in a tank with flowing seawater. Invert the dishes on a perforated table.
Bacterial mats in culture dishes	Bacterial mats overgrow polyps and serve as substrate for other fouling organisms.	Remove the mat with a small paintbrush and put the dishes in a tank with seawater flowing through it.
Unwanted fouling hydroids in polyp cultures	There are several invasive hydroids that will overgrow and kill desired polyps.	Gently remove the intruder hydroids with a small paintbrush.
Polychaete worms in culture dishes (fig. 11.4A)	I don't know what they do exactly, but when they are present polyps aren't happy.	Remove the worms with a pipette.
Small white flat worms in culture dishes (fig. 11.4B)	They crawl on top of the hydroids and eat their tentacles, killing them.	Remove the worms with a pipette.
Polyps of other species in culture dishes	Polyps of Aurelia and Cassiopeia (moon jellies and upside-down jellies, respectively) will overgrow, outcompete, and kill polyps of things you want.	Remove them with extreme prejudice.

Fouling organism	What they do	Possible solutions
Juvenile slender crabs (Cancer gracilis) hitchhiking on jellies.	They wander around on jellyfish hosts and eat parasites. If the crabs are too large, their pointy legs can tear holes in the jellies' bells.	Allow the crabs to remain on the jellies if they are smaller than one-inch in carapace width. If the crabs are one inch or larger in carapace width, remove them to avoid damage.
Small anemone hanging from the gonads of hydrozoan jellyfish (fig. 11.4C)	Planulae of the parasitic anemone Peachia are eaten by the host jelly. The parasitic anemone feeds on the host jellies gonads until the anemone is large enough to detach itself after which it sinks to the bottom to take up adult life.	Remove them with a forceps or just watch them for a while. It's a little weird, but an interesting living arrangement.
Barnacles (Alepas sp.) on medusae (fig. 7.12)	They live attached to jelly bells and eat zooplankton from surrounding water. In captivity barnacles grow very large very quickly and wear holes in the bell of the jelly as the jelly pulses and the barnacles whip around.	It is OK to allow the barnacles to remain attached while they are small, but remove them (using a forceps or tweezers) when the barnacles measure one inch or longer.
Hydroids (Obelia sp.) on medusae	They occur on wild medusae and grow as bushy clumps in the center of the bell of the host jelly.	They seem to have no ill effects on the host jelly and are an interesting symbiotic living arrangement.
Parasitic amphipods of medusae (fig. 11.4D)	They swim from one medusa to the next, eating holes and causing damage wherever they go. Sometimes they lay eggs in the host jelly; when the young amphipods hatch, they feed on their jellyfish host.	Remove them with extreme prejudice. Use a forceps.

Avoiding Culture Contamination

There are a number of things a jelly aquarist can do to limit the amount of contamination that occurs in jellyfish polyp cultures. Some of the major contaminants are fouling hydroids and polyps of *Aurelia* sp. One way contaminants are spread around your lab occurs at feeding time. I like to use turkey basters to feed *Artemia* nauplii to my cultures and exhibits. So it is important to never dip the turkey baster into the water of the various tanks when feeding cultures of multiple species. If you do dip the baster into the water, you can potentially spread tiny drifting reproductive material from one culture tank to the next.

Another useful tip is to always rinse your tools with fresh water between uses. Rinsing your tools is just good husbandry. It helps avoid salt buildup on the tools and keeps them in good working condition. Rinsing tools with fresh water helps combat contamination because it causes salt water–living fouling organisms to die a horrible osmotic death as their little cells swell up and burst in response to the fresh water.

One of the primary dietary components for cultured medusivores is moon jellies, either whole or chopped. Female moon jellies brood their planulae on their oral arms and release them into the water when the planulae are mature or if the female jelly is stressed. When an aquarist prepares chopped moons, diced moons, or even whole medusae, the planulae of the mother moon jelly are released into the water. When an aquarist feeds out chopped jellies, they are also in effect inoculating every tank they feed with

5

moon jelly planulae, which may develop into polyps. For this reason, it is again important to always rinse your tools. One should also consider having dedicated tools for specific jobs. For example, I use specific turkey basters and beakers to feed out chopped moons and nothing else. Using dedicated tools has gone a long way toward eliminating moon jelly polyp contamination in my cultures.

How to Get Your Resting Polyps to Produce Medusae

Table 11.2. Methods for strobilation induction and gonangium production in selected species.

Species	Maintenance Temperature °C	To induce strobilation
Northeast Pacific sea nettle Chrysaora fuscescens	14	Strobilate in episodic waves 2–3 times per year at 14°C; drop temperature to 8°C, strobilation in 5–6 weeks
C. colorata Puple stripe jelly	20	Drop temperature to 14°C, strobilation in 5–6 weeks
C. achlyos Black sea nettle	20	Drop temperature to 14°C, strobilation in 5–6 weeks
C. melanaster Black star nettle	20	Drop temperature to 14ºC for two weeks then bring temperature back up to 20°C, look for strobilation in 1–2 weeks
Cyanea capillata Lion's mane jelly	14	Strobilate on own in episodic waves 4–6 times per year at 14°C

Species	Maintenance Temperature °C	To induce strobilation
C. versicolor Lion's mane jelly (Gulf)	16	Ones from the Gulf of Mexico should be maintained at 28ppt and between 15°C–18°C
Phacellophora camtschatica Egg yolk jelly	14	Strobilate on own in episodic waves 4–6 times per year at 14°C
Aurelia labiata Moon jelly	14	Rarely strobilates at 14°C and salinity of 34 ppt, a salinity shift to 28 ppt required

From Juvenile Jelly to Early Medusa

Some jellyfish are easier to maintain than others. Fortunately, husbandry requirements for raising jellies are similar in most cases. For our purposes, we will consider three basic phases of jellyfish development in terms of their care requirements. Phase I are the newly released medusae, which generally measure from 2–10 mm in diameter. Phase II metamedusae range from 11–30 mm in diameter, and the phase III displayable medusae are larger than 30 mm in diameter. Jellies at different phases of development require different types of grow-out tanks and husbandry techniques.

Phase I starts when the jellies are released from their parent polyps (strobilae). During the first week or two, juvenile medusae of most jellyfish species may be kept in an eight-inch diameter glass culture dish filled with clean seawater and given daily water changes. When changing the water, have two dishes on hand: one with medusae and used seawater, and another with clean new seawater. Transfer the animals from the old dish to the new one using a pipette or small plastic spoon that has been heated and bent to a 90° angle.

Growing up in a dish filled with standing seawater is sufficient for some species of jellyfish, but other kinds of jellies require water movement in order to grow. Tentacles and mouth parts can stick to the bottoms of the dishes, causing problems because the jellies are unable to swim, exercise, or feed effectively. Fortunately, you can get juvenile jellies up and off the bottom of the dish by gently stirring the water with a magnetic stirrer or by using a shaker table. When using magnetic stirrers, I prefer plus-shaped ones rather than pill-shaped ones. To set the proper stirrer spin rate, adjust it such that the stirrer spins fast enough to get the jellies up and off the bottom of the dish but without rocketing them around. If a vortex forms in the center of the dish, the spinner is going too fast.

Another option for growing new medusae is to use is a shaker table. A shaker table is one on which you set juvenile jellyfish grow-out dishes. The table slowly and gently rocks back and forth. The gentle rocking motion keeps the jellies from sticking to the bottom of the dishes without bouncing them around. I have found shaker tables to be very effective for growing scyphozoan jellies (e.g., moon jellies and *Chrysaora* jellies) but not very good at growing hydrozoans (e.g., crystal jellies and cross jellies). Adjust

the table height such that dishes are partially submerged in a seawater bath so the dish temperature
remains constant.

But what if they don't grow?

1. If you started by trying to grow juvenile medusae
   in standing seawater you may need to use a stirrer instead. The reverse may apply if you started
   with a stirred dish and the jellies got beaten up.
   If neither of those methods worked, try using a
   shaker table.

2. If you were using a magnetic stirrer, was the spin
   rate of the stirrer adjusted properly? It should
   be adjusted such that the jellies are just lifted up
   and off the bottom of the dish but not bouncing
   around wildly.

3. You may not be feeding them enough food, or
   you may be fouling the water with too much food.
   Feed them a diverse diet, including enriched *Artemia* nauplii and rotifers if you have them. Are
   the jellyfish medusivores? If they are, there is a
   high probability that the juveniles should get
   diced moon jellies in their diet.

4. Are you being good about daily water changes?
   Has the salinity in the dishes been allowed to accidentally gradually increase? Has the temperature in the dishes remained constant?

Medusae reach phase II when they are about

8 mm in diameter. During phase II, I prefer to use one-foot diameter pseudokreisels or 5 × 5 ×7-inch screened-in flow-through tanks for most species. The specific tank types that work well for each growth phase for commonly grown jellyfish are given in chapter 7. Phase III medusae are display-sized ones that are generally larger than 30 mm in diameter. Instructions for particular tank designs for each species are also given in chapter 7.

There are some tricks you can use if you want to maximize jellyfish growth at phase III. First, moderately stock the display tank. If there are fewer jellies in the tank, individuals tend to get larger than when there are more jellies in the tank. Second, increasing temperature increases jellyfish growth … to a point. Jellyfish growth will be enhanced at the high end of their temperature operating range, but be careful not to exceed it! Feed the jellies two or three times per day at evenly spaced intervals (every eight hours). This allows the jellies enough time to digest their food, clear their guts, and get ready for the next feeding. The bottom line to healthy, happy jellyfish is to keep the flows adjusted properly, keep the tanks clean, and keep the jellies well fed.

Appendices

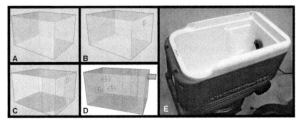

Figure A.1. Flow-through catch-tank made from a plastic rectangular "critter keeper." Illustration (E) shows a modified box-style tank made from a cooler. This inexpensive tank does a great job at growing moon jellies.

How to Build a Screened-in Flow-through Tank

1. Acquire a clear plastic rectangular box; they are available from most pet stores and are often sold as "critter keepers." An ice chest may also be used if aesthetics aren't an issue (fig. A.1E).

2. Decide where exactly you wish to drill the holes and put masking take on both sides of the holes before you drill them. This will help keep the plastic or acrylic from cracking while you drill.

3. Slowly and carefully drill one to three holes parallel to one another near the top of the tank (fig A.1B). Be very careful to not push too hard or spin the drill bit too quickly or the plastic will crack. Go slowly!

4. Measure and cut a rectangular shaped piece of nylon mesh screen (screen hole width about 250–500 microns).

5. Temporarily tape the screen in place (fig. A.1C).

6. Gently remove the tape on one side of the tank and glue the screen in place with aquarium-safe sealant. Repeat until all sides of the screen are glued in.

    ....
    A viewing window may be emplaced by cutting a hole in the side of the ice chest and gluing a piece of acrylic or glass inside, using aquarium-safe silicon. Be sure to cover all exposed edges with silicone to make sure jellies don't get cut by rough surfaces.
    ....

7. Allow to dry.

8. Water enters the large chamber on the left and passes through the screen first, then the outflow tube on the right side (fig. A.1D).

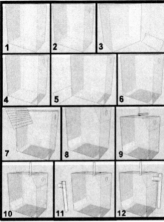

Figure A.2. Basic pseudo
kreisel construction.

How to Build a Basic Pseudokreisel

1. Start with a rectangular acrylic or glass box.

2. Use a hole saw to carefully cut a hole near the top
    on one side of the tank. The hole will serve as the
    return-to-reservoir drainage port. Remember to
    put masking tape on both sides of the hole before
    you cut it; taping both sides will help keep the
    acrylic from cracking.

3. Glue in one curved plastic bottom sheet.

4. Glue in the second curved plastic bottom sheet.

5. Cut and emplace an outflow cover screen. First
    glue the screen to a rectangular mounting bracket

and then glue the bracket to the inside walls of the tank (fig. A.3B through fig. A.3D).

••

If the system is destined to only house moon jellies, curved bottoms are a luxury but having them increases the versatility of the tank.

••

Figure A.3. Illustration (A) are spray bars shown at different angles [also (B), (C), and (D)]. Mounting bracket for pseudokreisel screen. Start with a flat sheet of 1/8-inch thick plastic (B). Cut a rectangular hole from the center, leaving about a one-inch margin (C). Using aquarium-safe silicone, glue plastic mesh screen material to the edges of the plastic mounting bracket (D).

6. Make and install a spray bar (fig. A.3A).

7. Using PVC, construct and mount the outflow return-to-reservoir line.

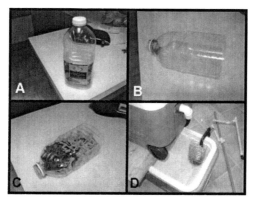

Figure A.4. Homemade trickle filter

How to Build a Trickle Filter

1. Start with a clean, recycled container.

2. Cut off the bottom.

3. Add plastic media for bacteria to live on. I like using plastic army men or pirates.

4. Mount the filter to the side of the reservoir. Water returning from the tank should pass through the trickle filter before entering the reservoir.

5. You can also include a piece of cotton-batting material across the top of the filter to catch large pieces of debris. Rinse this off as needed (or daily).

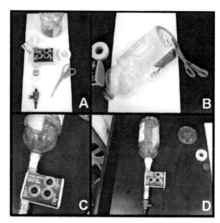

Figure A.5. Auto feeder construction.

How to Build an *Artemia nauplii* Autofeeder

1. Gather your supplies, all of which are to be found at the local hardware shop. You need aquarium-safe silicone, a clean, recycled plastic jug, scissors, a garden hose timer, a valve, and connecting hardware (to connect the valve to the timer).

2. Cut off the bottom of the recycled plastic jug. Be careful not to poke holes in your fingers!

3. Use the aquarium-safe silicone to affix the jug to the top end of the garden hose timer.

4. All done! Add the batteries and program the unit for three feeding events per day, evenly spaced eight hours apart. Add some zip ties to the top of the jug and hang it in a good location.

Conversions I Have Found Useful

Temperature

°Centigrade	0	5	10	15	20	25	30	35	100
°Fahrenheit		32	41	50	59	68	77	86	95	212

To convert °F to °C: $\dfrac{(°F - 32)}{1.8} = °C$

To convert °C to °F: $(°C \times 1.8) + 32 = °F$

Liquid measure

One cc = 1 mL
One liter = 1000 mL
One gallon = 3.8 L

Length

One µm = 1/1000 mm
One mm = 1/10 cm = 1000 µm
One yard = 91.44 cm
One inch = 2.54 cm

Water data

One gallon of seawater weighs about 8.5 lbs (3.86 k) and measures 231 inches cubed.

One cubic foot of seawater is about 64 lbs, 7.5 gal., 28.4 L, and 3785.4 cc

PLACES YOU CAN GO TO SEE JELLYFISH

AT THE TIME of my writing this paragraph, in April 2008, I knew of more than fifty zoos and aquariums in the world that were displaying jellyfish. In the continental United States, jellies were displayed in more than twenty-five states. Outside of the United States, I knew of at least fourteen different countries where jellyfish were displayed. A typical institution usually displays from three to seven kinds of jellyfish. The size of the place gives a clue about how many jellyfish species they may display. In general, larger institutions (with larger operating budgets and more time, space, and labor, etc.) can afford to display more kinds of jellyfish than do smaller places. The Monterey Bay Aquarium has been displaying jellyfish for more than twenty years, and aquarists there have developed many of the techniques used by the fifty other institutions listed below. Accordingly, the

Monterey Bay Aquarium has one of the world's largest permanent collections of living jellyfish polyps and medusae ever assembled. During my tenure, we typically displayed over twenty different kinds of jellyfish at a time. That huge effort was the labor of five full-time professional aquarists and a small army of volunteers. Below is a list of places you can go to see jellyfish.

California

Monterey Bay Aquarium, Monterey: More than twenty species
Cabrillo Marine Aquarium, San Pedro: Eight species
Long Beach Aquarium of the Pacific, Long Beach: Five species
Santa Monica Pier Aquarium, Santa Monica: One display
Stephen Birch Aquarium-Museum, La Jolla: Five species
Seymour Marine Discovery Center, Long Marine Lab, UC Santa Cruz: Three species
Chula Vista Nature Center, Chula Vista: Two species
Aquarium of the Bay, San Francisco: One display
Steinhart Aquarium, California Academy of Sciences, San Francisco: One display

Connecticut

The Maritime Aquarium, Norwalk: Five species
Mystic Aquarium, Mystic: Two species

Florida

The Florida Aquarium, Tampa Bay: Five species
Mote Marine Lab Aquarium, Sarasota: Four species
Seaworld Orlando, Orlando: Two species

Hawaii

Waikiki Aquarium, Honolulu: One display

Illinois

John G. Shedd Aquarium, Chicago: Six species
Brookfield Zoo, Chicago: One display

Kentucky

Newport Aquarium, Newport: Seven species

Louisiana

Aquarium of the Americas, New Orleans: Six species

Massachusetts

New England Aquarium, Boston: Fifteen species
Cape Cod Museum Natural History, Brewster: One display

Maryland

National Aquarium in Baltimore, Baltimore Calvert Marine
Museum, Solomons: One display

Michigan

John Ball Zoological Garden, Grand Rapids: One display

Nebraska

Omaha's Henry Doorly Zoo, Omaha: Two species

Nevada

Bellagio Hotel, Las Vegas: One display
Shark Reef, Mandalay Bay Resorts, Las Vegas: One display

New Jersey

Adventure Aquarium, Camden: Five species
Ocean Life Center, Atlantic City: One display

New Mexico

Albuquerque Biological Park, Albuquerque: Five species

New York

New York Aquarium, Brooklyn: Eight species

North Carolina

North Carolina Aquarium at Fort Fisher, Kure Beach: Two species

North Carolina Aquarium, Manteo: One display

Oklahoma

Oklahoma City Zoo, Oklahoma City: One display

Oregon

Oregon Coast Aquarium, Newport: Three species

Pennsylvania

Pittsburgh Zoo and PPG Aquarium, Pittsburgh: Two display

South Carolina

South Carolina Aquarium, Charleston: Three species

Ripleys Aquarium, Myrtle Beach: One display

Tennessee

Tennessee Aquarium, Chattanooga: Seven species

Texas

Texas State Aquarium, Corpus Christi: Seven species

Moody Gardens, Galveston: Three species

Dallas Aquarium at Fair Park Aquarist, Dallas: Two species

The Dallas World Aquarium, Dallas: One display

Dallas Aquarium at Fair Park, Dallas: One display

Virginia

Virginia Living Museum, Newport News: Two species

Virginia Aquarium, Virginia Beach

Washington

Seattle Aquarium, Seattle: One display
Pt. Defiance Zoo & Aquarium, Tacoma: One display

Washington DC

Smithsonian's National Zoo, Washington: One display

International

Melbourne Aquarium, Melbourne, Vic, Australia: Six species
Oceanis Australia Group, UnderWater World, Queensland, Australia
Atlantis Resort Nassau, Bahamas: Three species
Vancouver Aquarium, British Columbia, Canada: One display
Oresund Aquarium, Oresundsakvariet, Denmark: One display
Zoo-Aquarium   , Berlin, Germany: Seven species
Ocean Park Corporation, Aberdeen, Hong Kong: Five species
Acquario Di Genova, Genova, Italy: Four species
Aquamarine Fukushima, Fukushima, Japan
Acuario de Veracruz, Veracruz, Mexico: One species
Aquário da Madeira, Madeira, Portugal
Underwater World Singapore
Two Oceans Aquarium, Cape Town, South Africa: Four species
Seaworld, Durban, South Africa
Oceanario, Lisboa, Spain: Two species
The Deep, East Yorkshire, United Kingdom: Three species
Weymouth Sealife Park, Lodmoor Country Park, Dorset, United Kingdom: Eight species

GLOSSARY

algae : small aquatic plants found in both marine or freshwater environments

Artemia : small shrimp that are easy to culture and serve as a staple food item in the aquaculture industry

auto pilot : an aquarium may be set up so that it requires very little or no maintenance for short periods; an aquarium and its life-support system that is not receiving routine daily maintenance is said to be on auto pilot

bell : the main structural component of a jellyfish, it is primarily made up of a jelly-like matrix and is covered with a skin that is only two cell layers thick.

benthic : animals living on the sea floor are said to be benthic

cnida : the name for the penetrating dart produced by a cnidoblast

cnidoblast : a cell that generates the penetrating

darts, or cnidae, which jellyfish use to sting and inactivate prey; other types of cnidae are used for attachment, defense, prey capture, etc; once a cnida or nematocyst is discharged, a new one is generated by the parent cnidoblast cell

commensalism : a symbiotic association in which the symbiont receives benefit from the association but the host is neither harmed nor benefited

demersal : living near or around the bottom

ephyra/e : the term used for an immature, newly released scyphozoan jellyfish

gastrovascular cavity : gut or stomach, serves to digest food

gastrovascular canal/s : gut tubes leading from the central gut to the rest of the animal; the canals can be single tubes or highly branched (a condition known as anastomosed)

gastrozooid : the feeding polyp in a hydroid colony, also known as a hydranth

gastrulation : the embryonic process whereby embryonic germinal layers are formed

gonozooid : the medusa-producing polyp in a hydroid colony, also known as a gonangium

gut : the name used by zoologists to describe the digestive system and all of its components; also may be referred to alimentary canal in zoology

host : in a symbiotic association, usually the larger of the two organisms serving as a platform on which the symbiont lives

hydrotheca : the external tough coverings of hydroid colonies

hydrozoa : a class of jellyfish belonging to the phylum Cnidaria; benthic polyps are often arranged in colonies consisting of different types of polyps with different functions; medusae are produced by polyps called gonangia or gonozooids; food is captured by gastrozooids also known as hydranths; mature hydrozoan medusae are usually smaller than a baseball

husbandry : the science and field of animal care

kreisel : the name given to jellyfish-holding tanks having circular currents

manubrium : in hydrozoan jellyfish, the extension between the stomach and mouth that dangles down; it looks and functions similar to an elephant's trunk

medusae : the swimming phase of the jellyfish life history

medusivore : something that eats jellyfish

mouth arms : in scyphozoan jellyfish, the name given to the frilly lip-like extensions associated with the mouth and feeding

mutualism : a symbiotic association in which both the host and symbiont receive benefit from the association

nauplius/nauplii : a larval form of many crustaceans, including barnacles and shrimp; *Artemia* nauplii are a common live food used in aquaculture because they are commercially available and relatively easy to hatch and maintain

nematocyst : see cnidoblast

oral arms : see mouth arms

parasitism : a symbiotic association in which the

host is harmed and the symbiont receives benefit at the expense of the host

pelagic : living in the midwater, not associated with the bottom

polyp burn out : a situation in which scyphozoan polyps are maintained for extended periods at temperatures causing polyps to strobilate continuously without opportunity to regenerate a mouth in order to feed; the amount of viable ephyrae produced by polyps in this condition decreases over time

podocyst : a benthic-encysted, overwintering body of scyphozoan jellyfish polyps; they are asexually formed at the bases of polyps; if for some reason all of the polyps in a colony are wiped out new polyps may emerge from the podocysts when environmental conditions are favorable

polychaete : a type of marine segmented worm belonging to the phylum Annelida. They are distantly related to earthworms

polyp : the slang term used by cnidarian biologists for the benthic life history stages of jellyfish. The proper term for a scyphozoan polyp is a scyphistoma and the term for a hydrozoan polyp would be a hydranth or gonangium depending on its function within the colony

planula : larval form for members of the phylum Cnidaria, they are usually 2–3 mm long with visible ciliary action and the ectoderm and entodermal layers under a microscope

planulae : two or more specimens of planula

PVC : a primary building material used in a jelly life-support system

Pyrrhic truce/victory : a victory won at too great a cost to the victor

radial canal : in hydrozoan jellyfish, the gut tubes leading from the central stomach to the ring canal

rearing vessels : the tanks and dishes used to grow and keep jellyfish

ring canal : in hydrozoan jellyfish, the gut tube that encircles the perimeter of the bottom of the bell

rotifer : a very small animal with a ciliated ring around its mouth that wanders around eating things the size of bacteria; they are frequently used in aquaculture applications as live foods for animals with very small mouths

salinity : a measure of the "saltiness" of the water; typically, salinity is measured in ppt, parts per thousand, or PSU, practical salinity units

scyphistoma : the solitary benthic life history stage of a scyphozoan jellyfish; a scyphistoma looks like a miniature sea anemone about 1–3 mm tall with a single mouth encircled by a single whorl of tentacles; there is a column and a base from which, depending upon species, the scyphistoma may asexually reproduce by podocysts or side-budding

scyphozoa : a class belonging to the phylum Cnidaria; members of the class Scyphozoa have medusae with mouth arms and gonads generally arranged in a clover leaf pattern just under the apex of the bell; the polyps are generally solitary and undergo the process of strobilation, leading to the production of ephyrae that mature into medusae

slick : a place to look for jellyfish, the glassy signatures of the down-welling currents of Langmuir convection cells, also a good place to fish because copepods, a favorite food of fish, accumulate there

strobila : the benthic life history stage of a scyphozoan polyp that has elongated and formed ephyrae destined to be released; to strobilate is to undergo the process of strobilation or be in a state of becoming a strobila

symbiont : in a symbiotic association, the name given to either of the two associates

symbiosis : a biological arrangement wherein two or more different species live together; typically, there is a larger associate called the host and a smaller associate the symbiont; in the broadest terms, symbiotic associations may be beneficial, harmful, or neither for the host (mutualism, parasitism or commensalism, respectively)

tentacle : the primary morphological structure used by cnidarians for ensnaring prey, they are usually loaded with stinging cells and are sticky to the touch

theca : the chitinous outer covering of the benthic colonies of hydrozoan polyps

zorching : if jellies are placed in a tank containing residual bleach, the jellies will most likely shrivel up, retract their tentacles, and begin to die; jellies that have been thusly shocked have been "zorched"

BIBLIOGRAPHY

Abbot, D. P. *Observing Marine Invertebrates: Drawings from the Laboratory.* Stanford, California: Stanford University Press, 1987.

Albert, D. J. 2005. Reproduction and longevity of *Aurelia labiata* in Roscoe Bay, a small bay on the Pacific coast of Canada. *Journal of the Marine Biological Association of the United Kingdom* 85:575–581.

Arai, M. N. 1986. Oxygen consumption of fed and starved Aequorea victoria (Murbach and Shearer, 1902) (Hydromedusae). Physiological zoology 59(2):188–193.

———. 1991. Attraction of Aurelia and Aequorea to prey. Hydrobiologia 216/17(1):363–366.

———. 1997. *A Functional Biology of Scyphozoa.* London: Chapman & Hall.

Baker, L. D., and M. R. Reevel. 1974. Laboratory culture of the lobate ctenophore *Mnemiopsis mccradyi* with notes on feeding and fecundity. *Marine Biology* 26(1):57–62.

Bamstedt, U., M. B. Martinussen, and S. Matsakis. 1994. Trophodynamics of the two scyphozoan jellyfishes, *Aurelia aurita* and *Cyanea capillata*, in western Norway. *ICES Journal of Marine Science* 51(4):369–382.

Behrends, G., and G. Schneider. 1995. Impact of *Aurelia aurita* medusae (Cnidaria, Scyphozoa) on the standing stock and community composition of mesozooplankton in the Kiel Bight (western Baltic Sea) *Marine Ecology Progress Series* 127(1–3):39–45.

Boero, F. 1987. Life cycles of *Phialella zappai* n. sp., *Phialella fragilis* and *Phialella* sp. (Cnidaria, Leptomedusae, Phialellidae) from central California. *Journal of Natural History* 21(2):465–480.

Brodeur, R. D. 1998. In situ observations of the association between juvenile fishes and scyphomedusae in the Bering Sea. *Marine Ecology Progress Series* 163:11–20.

Brodeur R. D., H. Sugisaki, and G. L. Hunt. 2002.

Increases in jellyfish biomass in the Bering Sea: implications for the ecosystem. *Marine Ecology Progress Series* 233:89–103.

Buecher, E., C. Sparks, A. Brierley, H. Boyer, and M. Gibbons. 2001. Biometry and size distribution of *Chrysaora hysoscella* (Cnidaria, Scyphozoa) and *Aequorea aequorea* (Cnidaria, Hydrozoa) off Namibia with some notes on their parasite *Hyperia medusarum*. *Journal of Plankton Research* 23(10):1073–1080.

Caughlan, D. 1984. The captive husbandry of *Aurelia aurita*. *Drum and Croaker* 21(1).

Colin, S., J. H. Costello, and E. Klos. 2003. In situ swimming and feeding behavior of eight co-occurring hydromedusae. *Marine Ecology Progress Series* 253:305–309.

Colley, N. J., and R. K. Trench. 1983. Selectivity in phagocytosis and persistence of symbiotic algae by the scyphistoma stage of the jellyfish *Cassiopeia xamachana*. *Proceedings of the Royal Society of London* 219:61–82.

Costello, J. H., and R. Coverdale. 1998. Planktonic feeding and evolutionary significance of the lobate body plan within the Ctenophora. *Biological Bulletin* 195(2):247–248.

Costello, J. H., and S. P. Colin. 2002. Prey resource

use by coexistent hydromedusae from Friday Harbor, Washington. *Limnology and oceanography* 47(4):934–942.

Dawson, M. N., and W. M. Hamner. 2003. Geographic variation and behavioral evolution in marine plankton: the case of *Mastigias* (Scyphozoa, Rhizostomeae). *Marine Biology* 143:1161–1174.

Dawson, M. N. 2005. Morphological variation and systematics in the Scyphozoa: *Mastigias* (Rhizostomeae, Mastigiidae)—a golden unstandard? *Hydrobiologia* 537(1–3):185–206.

Esserl, M., W. Greve, and M. Boersma. 2004. Effects of temperature and the presence of benthic predators on the vertical distribution of the ctenophore *Pleurobrachia pileus*. *Marine Biology* 145(3):595–601.

Fitt, K. W. 1984. The role of chemosensory behavior of *Symbiodinium microadriaticum*, intermediate hosts, and host behavior in the infection of coelenterates and molluscs with zooxanthellae. *Marine Biology* 81(1):9–17.

Fukushi, K., N. Ishio, J. Tsujimoto, K. Yokota, T. Hamatake, H. Sogabe, K. Toriya, and T. Ninomiya. 2004. Preliminary study on the potential usefulness of jellyfish as fertilizer. *Bulletin of the Society of Sea Water Science, Japan* 58(2):209–217.

Gershwin, L. A. 1999. Clonal and population variation in jellyfish symmetry. *Journal of the Marine Biological Association of the United Kingdom* 79:993–1000.

Gershwin, L. A., and A. G. Collins. 2002. A preliminary phylogeny of Pelagiidae (Cnidaria, Scyphozoa), with new observations of *Chrysaora colorata* comb. nov. *Journal of Natural History* 36:127–148.

Gibbons, M. J., and S. J. Painting. 1992. The effects and implications of container volume on clearance rates of the ambush entangling predator *Pleurobrachia pileus* (Ctenophora: Tentaculata*). Journal of Experimental Marine Biology and Ecology* 163(2):199–208.

Greene, C. H., M. R. Landry, and B. C. Monger. 1986. Foraging behavior and prey selection by the ambush entangling predator *Pleurobrachia Bachei*. *Ecology* 67(6):1493–1501.

Greve, W. 1968. The "planktonkreisel", a new device for culturing zooplankton. *Marine Biology* 1(3):201–203.

Hamner, W., and I. R. Hauri. 1981. Long-distance horizontal migrations of zooplankton (Scyphomedusae: *Mastigias*). *Limnology and Oceanography* 26(3):414–423.

Hamner, W. M., and R. M. Jenssen. 1974. Growth, degrowth, and irreversible cell differentiation in *Aurelia aurita*. *American Zoologist* 14(2):833–849.

Hamner W. M. 1990. Design developments in the planktonkreisel, a plankton aquarium for ships at sea. *Journal of Plankton Research* 12(2):397–402.

Heeger, T., H. Moller, and U. Mrowietz. 1992. Protection of human skin against jellyfish (*Cyanea capillata*) stings. *Marine Biology* 113(4):669–678.

Hoff, F. H., and T. W. Snell. 2001. *Plankton Culture Manual*. Dade City, Florida: Florida Aqua Farms, Inc.

Kendall, J. L., and M. N. Badminton. 1998. *Aequorea victoria* bioluminescence moves into an exciting new era. *Trends in Biotechnology* 16(5):216–224.

Kinoshital, J., J. Hiromi, Y. Yamada. 2006. Abundance and biomass of scyphomedusae, *Aurelia aurita* and *Chrysaora melanaster*, and Ctenophora, *Bolinopsis mikado*, with estimates of their feeding impact on zooplankton in Tokyo Bay, Japan. *Journal of Oceanography* 62(5):607–615.

Kramp, P. L. 1961. Synopsis of the medusae of the world. *Journal of the Marine Biological Association of the United Kingdom* 40:469.

Larson, R. J. 1987. Respiration and carbon turnover

rates of medusae from the NE Pacific. *Comparative Biochemistry and Physiology* 87(1):93–100.

———. 1990. Scyphomedusae and cubomedusae from the eastern Pacific. *Bulletin of Marine Science* 47(2):546–556.

Lucas, C. H. 2001. Reproduction and life history strategies of the common jellyfish, *Aurelia aurita*, in relation to its ambient environment. *Hydrobiologia* 451:229–246.

Lynam, C. P., S. J. Hay, and A. S. Brierley. 2005. Jellyfish abundance and climatic variation: contrasting responses in oceanographically distinct regions of the North Sea, and possible implications for fisheries. *Journal of the Marine Biological Association of the United Kingdom* 85:435–450.

Martin, J. W., and H. G. Kuck. 1991. Faunal Associates of an undescribed species of *Chrysaora* (Cnidaria, Scyphozoa) in the Southern California Bight, with notes on unusual occurrences of other warm water species in the area. *Bulletin of Southern California Academy of Sciences* 90(3):89–101.

Martin, J. W., L. A. Gershwin, J. W. Burnett, D. G. Cargo, and D. A. Bloom. 1997. *Chrysaora achlyos*, a remarkable new species of scyphozoan from the Eastern Pacific. *The Biological Bulletin* 193(1)8–13.

Matsumoto, G. I. 1988. A new species of lobate ctenophore, *Leucothea pulchra* sp. nov., from the California Bight. *Journal of Plankton Research* 10(2):301–311.

McCloskey, L. R., L. Muscatine, L. and F. P. Wikerson. 1994. Daily photosynthesis, respiration, and carbon budgets in a tropical marine jellyfish (*Mastigias* sp.). *Marine Biology* 119(1):13–22.

Mills, C. E. 1993. Natural mortality in NE Pacific coastal hydromedusae: Grazing predation, wound healing and senescence. *Bulletin of Marine Science* 53(1)194–203.

Miyake, H., M. Terazaki, and Y. Kakinuma 2002. On the polyps of the common jellyfish *Aurelia aurita* in Kagoshima Bay. *Journal of Oceanography* 58(3):451–459.

Moe, M. 1992. *The Marine Aquarium Handbook, Beginner to Breeder*. Green Turtle Publications, Islamorada, Florida.

Morandini A. C., F. da Silveira, and G. Jarms. 2004. The life cycle of *Chrysaora lactea* Eschscholtz, 1829 (Cnidaria, Scyphozoa) with notes on the scyphistoma stage of three other species. *Hydrobiologia* 530/531:347–354.

Mutlu, E., and F. Bingel. 1999. Distribution and abundance of ctenophores, and their zooplankton food in the Black Sea. I. *Pleurobrachia pileus*. *Marine Biology* 135(4):589–601.

Nagabhushanam, A. K. 1950. Feeding of a ctenophore, *Bolinopsis Infundibulum* (O. F. Müller). *Nature* 184:829.

Pierce, J. 2005. A system for mass culture of upside-down jellyfish *Cassiopeia* spp. as a potential food item for medusivores in captivity. *International Zoo Yearbook* 39(1)62–69.

Purcell, J. E. 1991. A review of cnidarians and ctenophores feeding on competitors in the plankton. *Hydrobiologia* 217/17:335–342.

———. 1991. Predation by *Aequorea victoria* on other species of potentially competing pelagic hydrozoans. *Marine Ecology Progress Series* 72:255–260.

———. 2000. Aggregations of the jellyfish *Aurelia labiata*: abundance, distribution, association with age-0 walleye pollock, and behaviors promoting aggregation in Prince William Sound, Alaska, USA. *Marine Ecology Progress Series* 195:145–158.

———. 2003. Predation on zooplankton by large jellyfish, *Aurelia labiata*, *Cyanea capillata* and *Aequorea aequorea*, in Prince William Sound, Alaska. *Marine Ecology Progress Series* 246:137–152.

Purcell, J. E., and M. B. Decker. 2005. Effects of climate on relative predation by scyphomedusae and ctenophores on copepods in Chesapeake Bay during 1987–2000. *Limnology and Oceanography* 50(1):376–387.

Purcell, J. E. 2007. Environmental effects on asexual reproduction rates of the scyphozoan *Aurelia labiata. Marine Ecology Progress Series* 348:183–196.

Radwana, F. Y., L. A. Gershwin, and J. W. Burnett. 2000. Toxinological studies on the nematocyst venom of *Chrysaora achlyos. Toxicon* 38(11)1581–1591.

Rahat, M., and O. Adar. 1980. Effect of symbiotic zooxanthellae and temperature on budding and strobilation in *Cassiopeia andromeda* (Eschscholz). *Biological Bulletin* 159(2):394–401.

Raskoff, K. A., F. A. Sommer, W. M. Hamner, and K. M. Cross. 2003. Collection and culture techniques for gelatinous zooplankton. *Biological Bulletin* 204:68–80.

Russell, F. S. *The Medusae of the British Isles, Volume 1: Anthomedusae, Leptomedusae, Limnomedusae, Trachymedusae, and Narcomedusae*. Cambridge, England: Cambridge University Press, 1953.

———. *The Medusae of the British Isles, Volume 2: Pelagic Scyphozoa, with a supplement to Vol. I*. Cambridge, England: Cambridge University Press, 1970.

Rutherford, R. D., and E. V. Thuesen. 2005. Metabolic performance and survival of medusae in estuarine hypoxia. *Marine Ecology Progress Series* 294:189–200.

Schaadt, M., L. Yasukochi, L. A. Gershwin, and D. Wrobel. 2000. Husbandry of the black jelly (*Chrysaora achlyos*), a newly discovered scyphozoan in the eastern North Pacific Ocean. *Bulletin de l'Institut Océanographique* 20(1):289–296.

Shenker, J. M. 1984. Scyphomedusae in surface waters near the Oregon Coast, May-August, 1981. *Estuarine, Coastal and Shelf Science* 19(6):619–632.

———. 1985. Carbon content of the neritic scyphomedusa *Chrysaora fuscescens*. *Journal of Plankton Research* 7(2):169–173.

Strand, W. S., and W. M. Hamner. 1988. Predatory behavior of *Phacellophora camtschatica* and size-selective predation upon *Aurelia aurita* (Scyphozoa: Cnidaria) in Saanich Inlet, British Columbia. *Marine Biology* 99(3):409–114.

Suchman C. L., and R. D. Brodeur. 2005. Abundance and distribution of large medusae in surface waters of the northern California Current. *Deep-Sea Research II* 52:51–72.

Sugiura, Y. 1965. On the life-history of rhizostome medusae III. On the effects of temperature on the strobilation of *Mastigias papua*. *Biological Bulletin* 128:493–496.

Tamburri, M. N., M. N. Magdalena, and B. H. Robison. 2000. Chemically regulated feeding by a midwater medusa. *Limnology and Oceanography* 45(7):1661–1666.

Thuesen, E. V., D. Ladd, Rutherford, and P. L. Brommer. 2005. The role of aerobic metabolism and intragel oxygen in hypoxia tolerance of three ctenophores: *Pleurobrachia bachei, Bolinopsis infundibulum* and *Mnemiopsis leidyi*. *Journal of the Marine Biological Association of the UK* 85:627–633.

Titelman, J., L. Gandon, A. Goarant, and T. Nilsen. 2007. Intraguild predatory interactions between the jellyfish *Cyanea capillata* and *Aurelia aurita*. *Marine Biology* 152(4):745–756.

Towanda T., and E. V. Thuesen. 2006. Ectosymbiotic behavior of *Cancer gracilis* and its trophic relationships with its host *Phacellophora camtschatica* and the parasitoid *Hyperia medusarum*. *Marine Ecology Progress Series* 315:221–236.

Verdelr, E. A., and L. R. McCloskey. 1998. Production, respiration, and photophysiology of the mangrove jellyfish *Cassiopea xamachana* symbiotic with zooxanthellae: effect of jellyfish size and sea-son. *Marine Ecology Progress Series* 168:147–162.

Yip, S. Y. 1984. Parasites of *Pleurobrachia pileus* Müller, 1776 (Ctenophora), from Galway Bay, western Ireland. *Journal of Plankton Research* 6(1):107–121.

Werner, B. 1968. Polypengeneration und entwicklung von *Eutonina indicans* (Thecata-Leptomedusae). *Helgoland Marine Research* 18(4):384–403.

Widmer, C. L. 2004. The hydroid and early medusa stages of *Mitrocoma cellularia* (Hydrozoa, Mitro-comidae). *Marine Biology* 145:315–321.

———. 2005. Effects of temperature on growth of Northeast Pacific moon jellyfish ephyrae, *Aurelia labiata* (Cnidaria: Scyphozoa). *Journal of the Marine Biological Association of the United Kingdom* 85:569–573.

———. 2005. Jellyfish population trends in Southern Monterey Bay, California from 2000–2005. *Ecosystem Observations for the Monterey Bay National Marine Sanctuary* 11–12.

Widmer, C. L., J. P. Voorhees, M. A. Badger, J. W. Lambert, and N. M. Block. 2005. The effects of rearing vessels and laboratory diets on growth of Northeast Pacific jellyfish ephyrae (Cnidaria: Scyphozoa). *Drum and Croaker* 36:29–36.

Widmer, C. L. 2006. Lifecycle of *Phacellophora camtschatica*. (Cnidaria: Scyphozoa). *Invertebrate Biology* 125(2):83–90.

———. 2008. Life cycle of *Chrysaora fuscescens* Brandt, 1835 (Cnidaria: Scyphozoa) with a key to sympatric ephyrae. *Pacific Science* 62(1):71–82.

Wrobel, D., and C. E. Mills. 1998. Pacific coast pelagic invertebrates: a guide to the common gelatinous animals. Sea Challengers/Monterey Bay Aquarium, Monterey

PARTING WORDS

IT IS MY sincere hope that this brief tour of jellyfish husbandry provided some of the tools you were looking for. It is by no means an all-inclusive account, but I think it provides enough of the key elements to get started. Still, if there is any information that you found lacking, please send me your comments so I can be sure to include it in the second edition.

C. Widmer
P.O. Box 51304
Pacific Grove, Ca. 93950

INDEX

ABOUT THE AUTHOR

CHAD L. WIDMER has managed display and culture of jellyfish galleries at the Monterey Bay Aquarium, on Cannery Row in Monterey, California, for over seven years. His scientific work focuses on jellyfish life cycles and applied husbandry research and development. After serving in the US Army as an M-1 Abrams armor crewman (an M-1 tanker), he earned his master's and bachelor's degrees in marine biology from Humboldt State University, Arcata, California. He enjoys few things more than setting off car alarms with his Harley Davidson motorcycle.

Keep the shiny side up.
Made in the U.S.A.

CPSIA information can be obtained at www.ICGtesting.com
Printed in the USA
LVOW07s0026221014

409819LV00001B/46/P

9 781604 941265